CAMPAIGN 422

BOUVINES 1214

Philippe Augustus and the Battle for France

JAMES TITTERTON ILLUSTRATED BY GRAHAM TURNER

OSPREY PUBLISHING
Bloomsbury Publishing Plc
Kemp House, Chawley Park, Cumnor Hill, Oxford OX2 9PH, UK
Bloomsbury Publishing Ireland Limited,
29 Earlsfort Terrace, Dublin 2, D02 AY28, Ireland
1385 Broadway, 5th Floor, New York, NY 10018, USA
E-mail: info@ospreypublishing.com
www.ospreypublishing.com

OSPREY is a trademark of Osprey Publishing Ltd

First published in Great Britain in 2025

© Osprey Publishing Ltd, 2025

All rights reserved. No part of this publication may be: i) reproduced or transmitted in any form, electronic or mechanical, including photocopying, recording or by means of any information storage or retrieval system without prior permission in writing from the publishers; or ii) used or reproduced in any way for the training, development or operation of artificial intelligence (AI) technologies, including generative AI technologies. The rights holders expressly reserve this publication from the text and data mining exception as per Article 4(3) of the Digital Single Market Directive (EU) 2019/790

A catalogue record for this book is available from the British Library.

ISBN: PB 9781472868824; eBook 9781472868831; ePDF 9781472868800; XML 9781472868817

25 26 27 28 29   10 9 8 7 6 5 4 3 2 1

Maps by Bounford.com
3D BEVs by Paul Kime
Index by Sharon Redmayne
Typeset by PDQ Digital Media Solutions, Bungay, UK
Printed and bound in India by Repro India Ltd

Artist's note

Readers may care to note that the original paintings from which the colour plates in this book were prepared are available for private sale. The Publishers retain all reproduction copyright whatsoever. All enquiries should be addressed to:

Graham Turner, PO Box 568, Aylesbury, Bucks, HP17 8EX, UK
www.studio88.co.uk

The Publishers regret that they cannot enter into any correspondence regarding this matter.

Dedication

For Jack.

Knights are worth ten, horses are wild.

Osprey Publishing supports the Woodland Trust, the UK's leading woodland conservation charity.

To find out more about our authors and books visit www.ospreypublishing.com. Here you will find extracts, author interviews, details of forthcoming events and the option to sign up for our newsletter.

For product safety related questions contact productsafety@bloomsbury.com

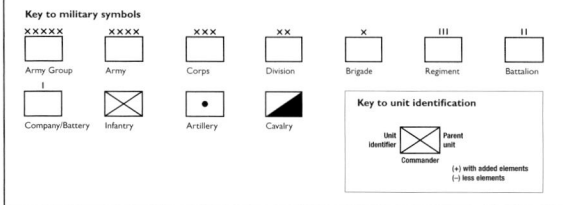

Front cover main illustration: King Philippe Augustus is saved from the foot soldiers, 27 July 1214. (Graham Turner)
Title page photograph: King Philippe Augustus offers to give up his crown at the battle of Bouvines. (Photo by Art Media/Print Collector/Getty Images)

CONTENTS

INTRODUCTION 5

CHRONOLOGY 9

OPPOSING COMMANDERS 10
Coalition . French

OPPOSING PLANS 22
Coalition . French

OPPOSING FORCES 26
Organization and finance . Troops – the knights (*milites, equites; chevaliers*) . Troops – the mounted serjeants (*servientes, satellites; sergants à cheval*) . Troops – the foot soldiers (*pedites*) . The face of medieval battle . Orders of battle

THE CAMPAIGN 42
The southern campaign – Poitou and Roche-aux-Moines . The northern campaign – the road to Bouvines . The battle – 27 July 1214

AFTERMATH 87
The consequences of Bouvines and Magna Carta

BIBLIOGRAPHY AND FURTHER READING 93

INDEX 95

Western Europe c.1200

INTRODUCTION

The battle of Bouvines (27 July 1214) is probably the most important battle in English history that English people do not know. In France, King Philippe II's victory holds a place equivalent to 1066 or 1415: a major milestone in the history and development of the French nation. Although the English contingent made up only a small part of the defeated army, that army – a coalition of German, Flemish and English magnates – was held together by money supplied by King John of England (r. 1199–1216). The campaign's failure left John humiliated and politically vulnerable at home. In June 1215, in an attempt to forestall the inevitable civil war, he submitted to the rebel barons' demands at Runnymede: Bouvines is the battle that resulted in Magna Carta and all that followed.

The Bouvines campaign was John's last great effort to recover the lands on the Continent that he had inherited in 1199 and lost to Philippe between 1202 and 1205. Since 1066, the kings of England had also been the dukes of Normandy, ruling a cross-channel 'Anglo-Norman' realm. John's father, Henry II (r. 1154–89), greatly increased these holdings by inheriting the county of Anjou from his father, Geoffroi, and then by his opportunistic marriage to Eleanor of Aquitaine, which added the county of Poitou and the duchy of Aquitaine to create what historians have called the 'Angevin Empire'. In truth, this was a disparate set of territories, each with its own laws and culture, united only by their fealty to the same man. Further complicating matters was the fact that, legally, Henry held these Continental lands as the vassal of the king of France, making him both their subject and their equal as an anointed king. The Capetian kings of France, first Louis VII (r. 1137–80) and then his heir Philippe II (r. 1180–1223), were determined to reduce the power of their over-mighty vassal, who commanded more influence and territory than they themselves. Henry and Richard I (r. 1189–99), John's elder brother, had managed to hold their 'empire' together through a combination of diplomacy, military action and sheer force of personality. However, Richard's unexpected death in 1199 at a minor siege in Limousin propelled John to the throne, where he proved wholly inadequate to the task.

A stamp issued by the French postal service in 1967. It depicts the essence of the Bouvines legend: the heroic Philippe Augustus, leading his people into battle, their enemies crumbling before their righteous fury. This legend would outlast even the monarchy and become a potent symbol of French nationalism. (DBI/Alamy Stock Photo)

The ruins of Château Gaillard, near Les Andelys, Normandy. Built on a 300ft limestone crag overlooking the Seine, Richard I spent £11,850 on its construction in 1196–98, more than he spent on all his English castles combined over his ten-year reign. (Andia/Universal Images Group via Getty Images)

In 1202, Philippe summoned John to his court to answer charges that John had illegally confiscated lands from the influential Lusignan family of Poitou and married Hugues de Lusignan's betrothed, the teenaged Isabella of Angoulême. John refused to attend, giving Philippe the opportunity to declare John's Continental lands forfeit to the French Crown. By year's end, Anjou, Maine and northern Poitou, their barons estranged by John's cruelty and arrogance, had all submitted to Philippe. In 1203, Philippe invaded Normandy, where the key stronghold of Vaudreuil surrendered without resistance. In August, Philippe laid siege to Château Gaillard, Richard I's 'Fair Castle of the Rock', the strongest fortress in Normandy and the key to its eastern defences. John attempted and failed to relieve the garrison, which nevertheless continued to hold out until the last defences were carried by storm in March 1204. This signalled the end of active resistance in Normandy. With John unwilling or unable to protect them, the other castles and towns of the duchy surrendered to Philippe without a fight. By 1206, John retained only a fragment of his Continental inheritance.

The next eight years saw a lull in Anglo-French hostilities, as John busied himself asserting his authority over the British Isles and Philippe was occupied by other political and diplomatic concerns. However, Philippe, aware of the growing resistance to John's rule across the Channel, planned to put an end to the Angevin dynasty for good and set his own son, Louis, on the throne of England. In April 1213, Philippe held a great council at Soissons, where he set in motion plans to invade England. John responded by summoning his barons to Dover to defend the realm and in May, in a diplomatic masterstroke, did homage to the papal legate for England, effectively placing the entire kingdom under the pope's protection. Undeterred, Philippe invaded the county of Flanders, John's ally, while assembling a huge fleet at Damme on the Channel coast to carry his army to England. He was thwarted by a sudden attack by a combined Anglo-Flemish force on 30 May that burned or captured over 300 ships. Philippe's invasion had come to nothing but John was unable to capitalize on the victory. He announced his intention to launch an invasion of his own into Poitou but the English barons would not follow him. Many had spent all their available funds standing in readiness to repel Philippe's invasion. The northern barons went even further, declaring their

Fortune's Wheel from the 'Carmina Burana', created c.1230 in southern Austria and now held in the Bavarian State Library. Fortune is depicted as a queen, enthroned at the centre of her wheel. As it turns, it raises some men up while casting down others. (Photo by Fine Art Images/Heritage Images/Getty Images)

obligations to John did not extend to campaigning overseas. Nevertheless, John sailed to Jersey, perhaps hoping to shame the barons into following him. None did.

In mid-November, John summoned his own war council at Oxford. At last, plans were put in place to launch a great campaign against Philippe. John's strategy was ambitious, drawing on both his financial might and a network of diplomatic alliances. A coalition of Philippe's enemies would attack on two fronts: John would lead an army into Poitou in the south, while his allies, including the German emperor himself, would attack from Hainaut in the north. Philippe would have to divide his forces to respond to both threats, leaving him vulnerable to a decisive stroke. Medieval writers often used the metaphor of 'fortune's wheel', which described life as a cycle in which men rose to glory and prosperity, only to fall into shame and poverty. At the beginning of 1214, Philippe appeared to be at the top of that wheel, with John on the downward arc. Perhaps now the wheel would turn once more.

CHRONOLOGY

1213

8 April	Philippe II holds a council at Soissons to prepare for the invasion of England
21 April	King John stations his army in Kent
15 May	John does homage to the papal legate for England
24 May	Fernando of Flanders renounces his fealty to Philippe
30 May	The French invasion fleet is burned at Damme
July	John fails to persuade his English barons to campaign in Poitou. Louis burns the city of Courtrai
September	Fernando burns Lille and Tournai
November	John holds a war council at Oxford

1214

January	Fernando does homage to John. Renaud de Dammartin attacks Cassel. Louis takes and burns Cassel and Steenvoorde
16 February	John lands at La Rochelle
4 March	John takes Milécu
23 March	Otto IV assembles his force at Aachen
17 May	John takes Miervant
13 June	John takes Nantes
17 June	John takes Angers
19 June	The siege of Roche-aux-Moines begins
2 July	Louis advances to Roche-aux-Moines; John retreats
9 July	John arrives at La Rochelle
12 July	Otto at Nivelles
23 July	Philippe leaves Péronne for Douai
26 July	Philippe at Tournai; the coalition at Mortagne
27 July	Battle of Bouvines
18 September	Truce between John and Philippe agreed at Chinon
13 October	John lands in England

OPPOSING COMMANDERS

Medieval armies were temporary entities, assembled only at need, governed by custom rather than doctrine and lacking a formal command structure. A good leader was expected to take advice from his followers; military command, like most contemporary politics, was built on consensus and interpersonal relationships. This was clearly demonstrated at Bouvines. On one side, Philippe of France, a respected and acknowledged leader, supported by trusted comrades who listened to the expert advice of his counsellor, 'Brother' Guérin. On the other, a coalition of relative strangers, united only by a shared paymaster and an antipathy for the French king. Emperor Otto might have been expected to act as commander-in-chief but there was no clear consensus among the various leaders, and a good deal of mistrust too. This lack of cohesion would be a decisive factor in the battle's outcome.

COALITION

While not quite the pantomime villain of stage and screen, contemporary sources depict **John, King of England (1167–1216)**, as a particularly unpleasant individual: cruel, lecherous, given to savage displays of anger, untrustworthy and paranoid. The English chronicler Matthew Paris declared: 'Foul as it is, hell itself is made fouler by John's presence'. His reputation as a military commander is not much better, although he suffers greatly by being compared to his brother, the legendary Richard the Lionheart. John occasionally displayed boldness and ambition as a commander but he lacked the charisma and political ability that encourage loyalty or secure lasting victory.

John's first recorded military action, in 1184, was an attack on his brother Richard. Their father, Henry II, had ceded the duchy of Aquitaine to Richard in 1172, on the expectation that Richard's elder brother, Henry, would inherit England and Normandy, thereby providing all the territories of the 'empire' with the personal government they required. The young Henry's death in 1183 forced the king to reconsider his plan. As eldest surviving son, Richard now stood to inherit the territories that should have gone to his elder brother, so the king ordered him to cede Aquitaine to John. Richard refused, as he regarded Aquitaine as his own personal possession, so Henry gave John, barely 17 years old, permission to take up arms and attempt to claim the duchy by force. He did not succeed. John was knighted the following year and despatched to pacify Ireland, only to return in September, having

The effigy on King John's tomb in Worcester Cathedral. The youngest of Henry II's sons, his own father reportedly gave him the epithet 'Lackland' in reference to his meagre Inheritance. By 1199, after a series of illnesses and violent deaths, John was left the sole heir to his father's 'empire'. (David Gee 4/Alamy Stock Photo)

offended and alienated many of the Irish princes. After his failed attempt to supplant Richard during his absence on crusade, John worked his way back into his brother's favour by turning on his former ally, Philippe Augustus, and fighting for Richard in his Norman campaigns in 1196–97.

John accomplished his greatest military feat in July 1202. His nephew, Arthur of Brittany, backed by Philippe, had rebelled and laid siege to John's mother, Eleanor, in the castle of Mirebeau in Anjou. John was 80 miles away at Le Mans when he heard the news. He arrived just two days later, an astonishingly quick forced march, taking the rebels by surprise and capturing over 200 knights and barons, including Arthur. His harsh treatment of his prisoners, however, (including Arthur's probable murder) only served to alienate the local nobility and convince them to transfer their loyalty to Philippe.

John's greatest military failure occurred only a year later, when he abandoned Normandy. The chronicler Roger of Wendover claimed that John was too lazy to fight, that he preferred to spend his mornings in bed with his new queen, but it is more likely that John mistrusted the Norman barons and feared capture, or worse, if he remained on the Continent. The barons had long resented Angevin rule and John's predecessors had gone to great lengths to retain the duchy. With John unable to either inspire their loyalty or compel their obedience, they had few qualms about giving their fealty to Philippe. The rest of John's reign was dedicated to raising the funds necessary to recover the lands he had lost and to retain those he still held. In 1206, he regained Gascony and southern Aquitaine from Philippe's ally, the kingdom of Castile. In 1210, he conducted a successful nine-week campaign in Ireland and, in 1211, led two expeditions into Gwynedd to check the Welsh prince Llywelyn ab Iorwerth. He also invested more than any previous king of England in the development of a navy to defend the south coast against the impending French invasion.

Richard I reportedly said of John: '[he] is not the man to win lands by force if there is anyone at all to oppose him'. The evidence suggests this was not quite fair. By 1214, John was a capable commander who could display real energy and strategic ambition. It was his political, rather than military, shortcomings that were to prove decisive in the Bouvines campaign.

To understand how **Otto IV, King of Germany and Emperor of Rome** (*c*.1175–1218) came to fight the king of France on behalf of the king of England, it is necessary to understand a little about the international politics of medieval Europe. When Emperor Heinrich VI died suddenly of illness in 1197, his son, Friedrich II, was only three years old and in the care of his mother, Constance, on Sicily. As German kings were technically elected rather than sons automatically inheriting from their fathers, as in England or France, and Germany urgently needed an adult ruler to maintain order, two new candidates were put forward by rival families. Friedrich's uncle, Philipp of Swabia, was the candidate for the Staufen dynasty. Opposing him was Otto of Brunswick, heir to the powerful Welf dynasty. The result was war between them and their supporters that would continue, intermittently, until 1215.

Otto was nephew to Richard I of England, having been raised at the Angevin court, and fought alongside Richard against Philippe Augustus in the 1190s. A contemporary chronicler called him 'arrogant and stupid' (*superbus et stultus*), although he conceded that Otto was taller and stronger than most men. Richard clearly had faith in him: he spent vast amounts supporting Otto's bid for the throne, hoping to secure Germany as an ally and a threat to France's eastern borders. In response, Philippe threw his support

A highly anachronistic portrait of Otto from 1839, which depicts him in late medieval plate armour, by Johann Christian Ludwig Tunica. Otto was raised at the court of his grandfather, Henry II of England, spoke fluent French and culturally had more in common with the English or French nobility than his German vassals. (Photo by Pictures From History/Universal Images Group via Getty Images)

behind the Staufen cause, effectively turning the German civil war into another front in the Angevin–Capetian conflict.

Richard's death in 1199 and John's defeats in 1204–05 seemed certain to end Otto's ambitions, only for his rival Philipp to be murdered over a personal quarrel in 1208. Otto capitalized on this turn of events by quickly betrothing himself to Philipp's daughter, Beatrix. Pope Innocent III (1161–1216) agreed to crown Otto as emperor, on the understanding that he would not attempt to take the kingdom of Sicily (which included large areas of southern Italy) from the young Friedrich. This would divide the empire between the Welf and the Staufen and end the geographical and political stranglehold that the German emperors had placed on Rome. Otto was crowned 21 October 1209 and almost immediately reneged on his promise. He proceeded through southern Italy, where the various cities willingly submitted to his authority, and made plans to invade Sicily proper. Innocent excommunicated him twice, in November 1210 and again in March 1211, which led to many of the German princes renouncing their fealty and electing Friedrich (now 17 and a viable ruler) as king. Otto returned to Germany and continued to fight the Staufen, with England and France once again sending money to support their respective candidates.

By 1214, Otto's cause was in serious decline. Although he still held his family lands in Brunswick and the upper Rhine, Friedrich's supporters controlled much of the rest of Germany. His decision to join John's coalition that year was probably motivated by a need to retain his uncle's financial support and the possibility that, if victorious, he might compel Philippe to end his support for the Staufen cause. The Bouvines campaign would determine the future of three dynasties: Angevin, Capetian and Welf.

The youngest of the coalition's leaders, **Fernando, Count of Flanders and Hainaut (1188–1233)**, third son of King Sancho I of Portugal (r. 1185–1211), had only been Count of Flanders for a few years when he rode to Bouvines. His aunt, Mathilde, dowager of Philip I of Flanders (d. 1191), had effectively purchased the county for him. She paid Philippe Augustus 50,000 livres to betroth Fernando to Jeanne, orphaned daughter of Baudouin IX of Flanders (d. 1205), whom Philippe had in his custody as Baudouin's lord. The pair were married in Paris in January 1212, where Fernando was also knighted by the French king and did homage to him for Flanders.

Philippe probably expected the young Portuguese count to be his pliable servant, but he overreached himself. Before Fernando and Jeanne were fully installed in Flanders, Philippe despatched his son Louis to violently seize the key border towns of Aire and Saint-Omer, ceded to Baudouin IX in 1200 as part of a peace treaty. Fernando was outraged but had no choice but to accept the situation for the time being. In April 1213, at the war council at Soissons, he demanded that Philippe return the towns in exchange for his help in the invasion of England. Philippe refused. In

The seal of Fernando, Count of Flanders. This is an 'equestrian' seal, depicting the owner as a mounted knight equipped for battle. Note how the artist has carved the shield in such a way that the viewer can clearly see that Fernando bears the Flemish arms: *or a lion rampant sable* (a black lion on a gold field). (SC/D/621 Archives Nationales, France)

Renaud de Dammartin's equestrian seal. Here the sculptor has depicted the rider travelling right to left, allowing them to centre the oversized shield decorated with the Dammartin arms: *argent, three bars azure, a bordure gules* (white with three horizontal blue bars and a red border). (SC/D/1059 Archives Nationales, France)

May, Fernando renounced his fealty to Philippe, citing the loss of Aire and Saint-Omer, and made a formal alliance with John. Philippe invaded Flanders and was besieging Ghent when his invasion fleet was burned at Damme.

In the year that followed, Flanders was devastated as Philippe and Fernando conducted a war of raid and counter-raid. In September 1213, Fernando took and burned the cities of Lille and Tournai, then spent the following spring ravaging the land of the Count of Guines. In June 1214, just before the Bouvines campaign, he laid siege to Aire itself, threatening to carry the war into Artois and beyond.

The wealthy county of Boulogne occupied a vital strategic position on the Channel coast between Normandy and Flanders. By abducting and marrying the widowed countess Ida (allegedly with her cooperation) in 1191, **Renaud de Dammartin, Count of Boulogne (*c*.1165–1227)**, son of the Count of Dammartin, made himself one of the great magnates of north-western Europe. This suited Philippe Augustus, as the counts of Dammartin were his vassals and Renaud's coup moved Boulogne away from the counts of Flanders and into the French sphere of influence. On his return from the Third Crusade in 1192, he retroactively annulled Renaud's first marriage and received his homage for Boulogne, along with a hefty financial settlement above and beyond the normal relief due from a vassal receiving a new fief.

Renaud proved a ruthless politician, perfectly willing to change allegiance in order to further his own ambitions. In 1197–98, he joined Richard I's alliance against Philippe in return for lands in England. In 1200, he abandoned John and went back to Philippe, betrothing his daughter to one of Philippe's sons in August 1201. Renaud fought with great distinction in the conquest of Normandy. At the siege of Château Gaillard, alongside Guillaume des Barres and Gautier de Châtillon (his future opponents at Bouvines), he rallied the common soldiers to defend the French siege camp against the Angevin relief force. After the victory, Philippe rewarded him with the Norman counties of Varenne, Aumale and Mortain.

A few years later, territorial conflict with the de Dreux family pushed Renaud back into the Angevin coalition. In 1211, when Philippe refused to side with him against Philippe, Bishop of Beauvais, Renaud took up arms against the bishop. King Philippe responded with force and Renaud, unable to resist him alone, fled east to the imperial county of Bar. The following year, through the intercession of Otto IV, Renaud was reconciled to John, doing homage to him in May 1212 at London and agreeing a pact of mutual assistance against Philippe. He was one of the leaders of the force that burned Philippe's fleet at Damme in 1213 and fought alongside Count Fernando in Flanders in early 1214.

The dukes of Brabant (also known as the dukes of Louvain) were among the most powerful lords in the Low Countries, second only to the counts of Flanders, ruling a sprawling territory between the Scheldt and the Rhine.

The effigy on William Longespée's tomb, Salisbury Cathedral. One of Henry II's many illegitimate children, William served his brothers as a senior diplomat and military commander. This effigy is a superb example of contemporary armour. (Salisbury Cathedral, photographer Finbarr Webster)

Hendrik I, Duke of Brabant (d. 1235) was an expansionist, with designs on the prince-bishopric of Liège on his eastern borders, through which he could control the trade along the Meuse valley between Cologne and Bruges. To this end, he sought the aid of Philippe Augustus, pledging loyalty to him in 1205 and marrying his widowed daughter, Marie, in April 1213.

In October of that same year, his invasion of Liège was defeated by an alliance between Hugues, Bishop of Liège, Fernando of Flanders and Hendrik's own nephew, the Duke of Limburg. As part of the peace settlement, Hendrik was required to hand over his two sons to Fernando as hostages. This gave him a powerful incentive to align himself with Fernando and, by extension, John's coalition against Philippe. This suited Otto IV, as Hugues was a dedicated supporter of his dynastic rivals, the Staufen, and Brabant would be a valuable ally in his war with Friedrich II. The new political status quo was secured by Otto's marriage to Hendrik's daughter, Maria, on 19 May 1214 (his first wife, Beatrix, had died shortly after their wedding in 1208). This was how Hendrik found himself marching against his father-in-law alongside Fernando of Flanders and Hendrik of Limburg, whom he had fought against in pitched battle less than a year before. Yet his membership of the coalition was, at best, a matter of expediency: he wanted to remain on good terms with both Philippe and Otto, with a view to using one or the other to help him further his personal designs against Liège. This conflict of interest would be an important factor in the campaign of July 1214.

John took the majority of his English troops to Poitou in 1214 but a handful were entrusted to his representative in the coalition army, his half-brother **William Longespée, Earl of Salisbury (d. 1226)**. William was one of Henry II's numerous illegitimate children and was widely acknowledged as such: his coat of arms, six gold lions on a blue field (*azure six lions rampant or*), resembled that of Henry's father, Geoffroi, Count of Anjou. His cognomen 'Longespée' (longsword) was derived from either his great height or his skill in battle. He served his brothers Richard and John as a senior military commander in Normandy, Brittany, Gascony and Ireland. Richard rewarded him in 1196 with marriage to Ela, heiress to the earldom of Salisbury, but he never received substantial estates of his own: he was far more useful as a royal agent, acting as either soldier, diplomat or administrator as required. In May 1213, he captained the expedition that burned Philippe Augustus's invasion fleet off Damme and continued to fight alongside Fernando of Flanders into 1214.

FRENCH

Philippe II's Great Seal, used to authenticate documents issued by the royal court. It depicts Philippe enthroned in majesty, crowned and holding a sceptre and a fleur-de-lys. It is a symbolic portrait, unlikely to bear any resemblance to the actual man. (SC/D/38 Archives Nationales, France)

Like with many individuals from this period, we know relatively little about **Philippe II Augustus (1165–1223)** as a person: pen portraits of royalty (often simply a list of conventional virtues) were intended to flatter rather than record. Philippe appears to have been a severe and pious individual, who forbade swearing at court and was noted for his antipathy towards minstrels and other entertainers. A highly skilled diplomat and statesman, he is famous for his administrative reforms as much as his military conquests. His contemporary biographer, Rigord, a brother of the royal monastery of Saint-Denis, gave him the imperial epithet *Augustus* (majestic, venerable) before he had turned 40. He certainly did not lack physical courage, fighting hand-to-hand at Bouvines, and could be a bold and dynamic general. His greatest strength as a commander, however, was in besieging fortifications, the predominant mode of warfare in the High Middle Ages, and he was always

The 'Old Town' of Acre, Israel. Philippe played a key role in taking the city from Saladin's garrison as part of the Third Crusade but his decision to return to France afterwards overshadowed this substantial achievement. (Photo by MENAHEM KAHANA/AFP via Getty Images)

accompanied on campaign by a cadre of expert engineers. In an era in which military technology greatly favoured the defender, Philippe was able to storm and capture some of the greatest strongholds in Europe.

In accordance with French royal tradition, Philippe was crowned king in 1179 while his father, Louis VII, was still alive, to ensure a smooth succession after his death. The early years of his reign saw him campaigning in Flanders, Berry and the Norman Vexin. In 1185, he besieged the castle at Boves (in modern Hauts-de-France), broke down the gate and carried the fortress by storm. In 1188, together with Richard I of England and Philip I of Flanders, Philippe took the cross, vowing to travel to the Holy Land and recover the city of Jerusalem from Saladin. Various factors, not least mistrust of Richard, delayed his departure to 1190. After wintering in Sicily, in April 1191, Philippe arrived at the siege of Acre, the 'bridgehead' for the crusade, two months ahead of Richard, who had delayed his journey to conquer Cyprus. Philippe's engineers proved instrumental in undermining the city walls and facilitating a series of assaults over the summer months. When he fell ill, Philippe had himself carried to the front line in a litter, where he sat, under a shelter, shooting at the garrison with a crossbow. Richard finally arrived in June and the garrison surrendered to the combined crusading forces on 12 July. Philippe, still very ill, left the Holy Land a few weeks later, although the majority of his troops remained, under the command of Hugues III, Duke of Burgundy.

Philippe was back in France by December 1191, where he took advantage of Richard's absence to launch a series of invasions into Normandy, Touraine and Aquitaine, enthusiastically supported by Richard's brother, John. Upon his return in 1194, after a spell in the prisons of the German emperor, Richard set about reclaiming the territory Philippe had seized in his absence.

Philippe suffered a series of embarrassing, if not decisive, defeats in a period of intermittent warfare that lasted until Richard's death in 1199. At Fréteval in July 1194, Richard overtook Philippe's rearguard and seized his baggage, including the French royal seal and archives. Philippe was forced to hide in a nearby church in order to avoid capture.

It is impossible to say what might have happened had Richard lived beyond 1199 to continue the conflict. As it was, Philippe was able to take advantage of John's shortcomings and conquer Normandy in less than two years. His siege of Château Gaillard in 1203–04 was an exemplary display of medieval siege tactics, combining bombardment, mining, infiltration and a tight blockade to wear down the English garrison. From hiding from Richard in a wayside church to planning an invasion of England, by 1214 Philippe was the ascendant power in Western Europe.

Philippe II's heir and only child by his first queen, Isabelle of Hainaut, was **Louis, Count of Artois (1187–1226)**. In 1209, on the Feast of Pentecost, he was knighted at Compiègne alongside his cousins, Robert III and Pierre de Dreux. This ceremony marked Louis's entry into manhood. Although he was not crowned during his father's lifetime (a break with French custom), he still acted as Philippe's trusted commander and representative. In 1212, shortly after the marriage of Fernando of Portugal to Jeanne of Flanders, Philippe despatched Louis and the de Dreux brothers to attack and capture the towns of Aire and Saint-Omer in Artois, which Louis claimed by right of his mother. This act, which John W. Baldwin described as 'brutal opportunism', alienated Fernando from Philippe and eventually pushed him into John's coalition.

In 1213, Louis took the cross, intending to go south and fight in the ongoing crusade against heresy in the Languedoc region of southern France, but his father forbade it, ordering him instead to prepare to lead an invasion of England. Philippe intended to depose John and place Louis on the English throne, which the pope had declared forfeit after John refused to accept his preferred candidate as Archbishop of Canterbury. Philippe took steps to ensure that his son did not set himself up as a potential rival, however. At the council at Soissons, Louis swore not to distribute any English land or receive homage from the English barons without Philippe's consent. After the loss of the French fleet at Damme in May 1213, Louis remained with his father in Flanders, prosecuting the war against Fernando. In July, he burned the city of Courtrai in retaliation for the defiance of other Flemish cities and, in January 1214, he likewise took and burned the towns of Cassel and Steenvoorde.

Although Philippe was the acknowledged leader of the French army at Bouvines, it is clear from the testimony of Guillaume le Breton, the only eyewitness chronicler of the battle, that the army's strategy was determined by a cleric, **'Brother' Guérin, bishop-elect of Senlis**. Nothing is known of Guérin's history prior to his appearance in the records of Philippe's court in 1197, where, according to Baldwin, he acted as 'a wide-ranging, omnicompetent administrator', whose talents encompassed finance, diplomacy and the law. Guillaume le Breton tells us that he had been a member of the Knights Hospitaller, one of the military orders established to protect the kingdom of Jerusalem, before he joined the royal court, and that he continued to wear their distinctive black habit, for which he was known as 'Brother'. He was elected to the bishopric of Senlis in 1213 after the previous incumbent retired due to excessive age and obesity. This was probably a reward from the king for Guérin's role in reconciling him with his estranged queen, Ingeborg, that same year. At the time of Bouvines, Guérin had not yet been formally ordained, hence he was referred to as 'the bishop-elect'.

In addition to his formidable administrative talents, Guérin appears to have been an experienced and respected military commander. It was he who had the presence of mind to scout the enemy advance on the morning of 27 July, he who advised Philippe to stand and give battle and he who organized the deployment of the crucial French right wing. Guillaume le Breton described him as a 'very bold man, of prudent and remarkable counsel, and very skilled at predicting future events'.

Anybody who studies the French army at Bouvines cannot fail to notice the wide-ranging influence of the de Dreux family. Not only did the patriarch, Robert II, command the left wing, he was related by blood or marriage to a number of other key individuals who fought alongside him.

Robert I de Dreux (d. 1188) was a younger son of Louis VI of France, making him brother to Louis VII, from whom he received the lordship of Dreux, located west of Paris, in 1152. In his later years, he acted as an advisor to his nephew, Philippe Augustus. His son, **Robert II (d. 1218)**, continued this close relationship with his royal cousin. He took the cross and accompanied Philippe on the Third Crusade, fought for him against Richard the Lionheart in the 1190s and then at the siege of Les Andelys in 1203. It is a mark of the king's trust and confidence that he gave him command of the left wing of the army at Bouvines, where he was opposed by two highly experienced commanders in William of Salisbury and Renaud de Dammartin. Robert II's eldest son and heir, **Robert III (d. 1234)**, continued the family tradition of close relations with the royal family, being knighted alongside Philippe's son Louis in 1209. Philippe Augustus clearly had great confidence in Robert III, entrusting him with the defence of the port town of Nantes in southern Brittany alongside his brother, Pierre, who held the duchy of Brittany by right of marriage.

Robert II was accompanied at Bouvines by his brother **Philippe, Bishop of Beauvais (d. 1217)**. Although technically forbidden from fighting by Church law, many medieval bishops were active military commanders due to their

An engraving, based on an imagined portrait of Louis as king of France, painted c.1837 by Henri Lehmann. He was an active soldier, both under his father and as king in his own right. His reign was cut short when he contracted dysentery on crusade in the Languedoc and died in November 1226. (Photo by Hulton Archive/ Getty Images)

A 19th-century engraving of two Knights Hospitaller, or members of the Order of the Knights of the Hospital of Saint John of Jerusalem. It is likely that Philippe worked closely with members of the order during the siege of Acre and this is how 'Brother' Guérin came to enter his service. (Photo by Buyenlarge/Getty Images)

responsibilities as major landowners and royal servants. Philippe de Dreux appears to have had few scruples about taking part in martial exploits, or much else. Upon returning from the siege of Acre, he spread rumours that Richard the Lionheart had plotted to murder Philippe Augustus while they were on crusade, then acted as Philippe's chief negotiator with Emperor Heinrich VI to keep Richard imprisoned for as long as possible. An active captain in the wars over the Vexin, he was captured in battle by Richard's captain Mercadier in May 1197. When the pope demanded that Philippe be released, Richard sent him the 'habit' that the bishop had been wearing when he was captured: a mail hauberk. It was not until June 1200 that John was finally persuaded to free Philippe as part of the Treaty of Le Goulet, albeit for the substantial sum of 2,000 silver marks.

The de Dreux extended their influence even further by marrying into many of the noble families of northern and eastern France. Robert I's marriage to Agnes de Baudemont-Braine gave the family the lordship of Braine, making them vassals to the counts of Champagne as well as the king of France. In 1210, Robert III married Aliénor de Saint-Valéry, whose brother, Thomas, fought alongside Robert II at Bouvines. Henri, Count of Bar, was Robert II's son-in-law and Gautier, Count of Saint-Pol, who fought with great distinction on the French right wing, was a de Dreux cousin via his mother, Adèle. Like most aristocratic marriages, these were first and foremost political alliances and helped to give the French army coherence and a sense of common purpose. The leading nobles were bound to one another and, ultimately, to the French Crown through the extended de Dreux family. The king's prosperity was their prosperity: if he was weakened, or even dethroned, then they too would suffer, losing their connection to the centre of power and patronage. This was a powerful motivation to fight at Bouvines, whereas the coalition fought at great risk for only the promise of future gains.

The reverse side of Robert II de Dreux's seal, displaying the de Dreux coat of arms. Later armorials (visual records of coats of arms made by heralds) recorded the tinctures (colours): *chequy or and azure, a bordure gules* (yellow and blue check with a red border). (SC/D/721/bis Archives Nationales, France)

OPPOSING PLANS

Students of 13th-century military history who wish to recreate a commander's plan for a given campaign or battle face a number of very serious obstacles. First and foremost is the lack of surviving documentation. Medieval Europe was primarily an oral culture and we lack the manifests, written orders, letters and communiqués that enable historians of later periods to reconstruct commanders' intentions. When contemporary narratives discuss strategy or intention, it is always with the benefit of hindsight and usually with considerable bias in favour of one side or the other. As we shall see, Guillaume le Breton presents a detailed list of the coalition's objectives in the northern theatre of the campaign but he had clear political and rhetorical reasons for making them as grandiose as possible. To recreate a medieval commander's plans at the outset of a campaign, we must infer their intentions from the actions they took and what could realistically be achieved by comparing it to other contemporary campaigns.

This is not to say that medieval commanders did not plan for campaigns or take advice on the best course of action. If anything, medieval campaigns are notable for the large number of councils held, even in moments of great urgency. As previously mentioned, armies of this period were temporary assemblies where the relationship between commanders and their subordinates was defined by existing socio-political relationships (or lack thereof), not modern concepts of military discipline or hierarchy. Authority was partly a matter of consensus between ruler and ruled and lords were expected to seek advice from their vassals. Indeed, it is common for chronicle narratives of this period to blame military defeat on a commander failing to take counsel before acting, or ignoring good advice when it was offered.

COALITION

The coalition's plan appears to have been very ambitious. Two armies were to operate in two different theatres separated by hundreds of miles. King John would command the southern theatre. Landing at La Rochelle, he would reestablish his authority over the county of Poitou, gathering additional forces as the local barons rallied to him as their rightful lord. From there he would march north, to his ancestral seat in the county of Anjou. It is unclear what the next step would be but he seems to have intended to carry his offensive north of the Loire, perhaps into Maine or Normandy. In a letter written at Parthenay in May 1214 describing his successes in the region,

The Porte Saint-Jacques at Parthenay, where John wrote his letter boasting that he intended to march beyond Poitou and strike at Philippe. The gatehouse was built in the early 13th century and restored in the 19th. (P. Eoche/Getty Images)

he concluded: 'But now God's grace has given to us an opportunity to rise against our mortal enemy, the king of the French, beyond Poitou'.

It is more difficult to reconstruct exactly what the northern army's objectives were. We can be reasonably sure that the leaders did not intend to seek a set-piece battle with Philippe of the kind that they eventually fought at Bouvines. Pitched battles were very rare events in the High Middle Ages. Richard the Lionheart only fought one in his whole career and his father Henry II, a commander of great reputation, never fought one. The risks associated with committing to such an engagement were very high. Armies of this period were relatively small and, once the fighting started, commanders had very limited control over their forces. Moreover, commanders were expected to lead from the front, fighting in the thick of the melee where there was a good chance they would be wounded or even killed. Commanders (and their propagandists) sometimes claimed that they were seeking battle, only to be thwarted by adverse circumstances or the enemy's reluctance to fight, but the weight of evidence suggests that these set-piece encounters usually occurred when one side was desperate for a decision or someone made a mistake. At Bouvines, it was arguably both.

Labourers dig a trench to defend a stronghold. Much of medieval warfare was taken up with blockading and bombarding strongholds. Counterweight stone throwers of the kind depicted (r) were first introduced to Western Europe around the time of Bouvines. (The Master and Fellows of Trinity College, Cambridge, MS O.9.34 f. 26r)

Guillaume le Breton depicts the leading members of the coalition seeking just such a battle, with the intention of deposing Philippe Augustus and carving up France between them. In the *Philippide*, Otto declares that the kingdom would be divided as follows: Renaud de Dammartin would have Péronne and the Vermandois, Fernando of Flanders would have Paris, William of Salisbury would have Dreux and Otto himself would have Sens and all the land between the Yonne and the Loing. It should be remembered that Guillaume was not present at any of the coalition's councils and, more importantly, was writing after the battle in order to praise Philippe and denigrate his enemies. It fitted his general depiction of Philippe as a humble and pious man, in contrast to the arrogant and anti-clerical Otto, to depict the coalition's leaders making these grand claims before their campaign had even begun.

If the coalition was not seeking a battle, then what was its goal? It is likely that the plan fell within the parameters of a typical campaign of this time and place: to devastate the land and capture towns and castles. Medieval warfare was characterized by raid and counter-raid, as armies attacked their enemies' economic base, meaning agricultural land. Burning farms and villages, carrying off livestock or peasant labourers and destroying crops were the foundation of any medieval campaign and the surest way to damage the enemy's ability to keep their army in the field. Even a small garrison of cavalry, operating out of a castle or fortified town, could cause significant damage to the surrounding area or harass an army's line of supply. Such garrisons had to be contained or eliminated if a commander wished to carry their offensive any distance beyond their own borders. The result was extensive siege warfare, with armies preferring to withdraw and circumvent one another when threatened. Direct attacks were normally made only when one commander was confident that they had a decisive advantage and they were quite prepared to use stratagems to create such a situation, whether by spreading false intelligence, laying ambushes or attacking an unsuspecting enemy under cover of darkness.

If one looks at the movements of the coalition army in the summer of 1214, it appears that it intended to campaign beyond the borders of Flanders and Hainaut. Plausible targets include Arras in Artois or key cities on the Somme such as Amiens or Corbie. The devastation inflicted by the coalition army, plus the loss of revenue from these wealthy cities, would harm Philippe both economically and politically. Defending one's lands and subjects was a king's primary purpose: if he failed, his subjects might be tempted to renounce their fealty and seek another, more capable ruler. The coalition's overall goal was probably not to permanently occupy the strongholds taken, or to depose Philippe, but to force him to negotiate according to their terms. We can only speculate what their demands might have been but they would surely have included the restoration of some, if not all, of John's Continental lands, territorial concessions to both Fernando of Flanders and Renaud de Dammartin and a punishing series of financial reparations.

The great strength of the coalition's plan was that they could attack on two fronts. Philippe would be forced to divide his forces or risk leaving one of the armies to roam unchecked through France. This meant that each army would be facing a diminished French force, less inclined to confront the coalition or risk battle. If it should happen that John or Otto found themselves with a clear advantage, either in numbers or position, and the opportunity to inflict a decisive blow through battle, then all the better. Prisoners would provide significant leverage in the eventual negotiations: a captive king most of all.

FRENCH

As the invaded power, Philippe Augustus's role in the Bouvines campaign was necessarily reactive. The coalition had chosen the theatres and it was up to him to respond as best he could. Upon learning that John had invaded Poitou, Philippe reinforced the garrisons of his castles in Vermandois and Boulogne to protect Paris from an attack from the north, then marched south with his field army. In April, at Châteauroux, Philippe made the decision to divide his forces, as the coalition had likely anticipated he would. The smaller part, including about a third of his knights plus auxiliaries, was to remain in Poitou under his son Louis and Henri Clément, Marshal of France. The remainder would return north with Philippe to counter the coalition's offensive into Picardy.

As with the coalition, it is unclear precisely what Philippe or Louis intended to do but it is unlikely that either sought a pitched battle, as the royal chronicler Guillaume le Breton would later claim. It is more likely that they planned to adopt the usual strategy of a medieval army defending its lands: shadow the enemy at a safe distance and attack its supply lines, while leaving nothing but scorched earth ahead of him. With care and a little good fortune, the enemy would be unable to make any significant advances and would be forced to retire in the autumn, when bad weather and lack of supplies would make it almost impossible to keep an army in the field.

Illumination depicting Louis and his wife, Blanche of Castile, at their coronation. Louis was a capable and enthusiastic soldier, hence Philippe delegating command of the southern front to him in 1214, but Blanche was to prove the more formidable ruler as queen-regent of France. (Photo by API/Gamma-Rapho via Getty Images)

OPPOSING FORCES

At first sight, it would have been very difficult to differentiate between the two armies that fought at Bouvines. They both came from the same north-western European civilization, used the same equipment and tactics, followed the same religion and shared similar cultural values. A number of the principal commanders had previously fought alongside, or were related to, members of the opposing army: both Renaud de Dammartin and Hendrik, Duke of Brabant, were related to Philippe Augustus by marriage. For these reasons, it would be redundant to consider 'the French army' and 'the coalition army' as separate entities. Instead, the organization, equipment, tactics and military ethos of the High Middle Ages will be considered as a whole, while noting the occasional significant differences between the two armies at this specific battle.

ORGANIZATION AND FINANCE

Philippe Contamine described Philippe Augustus's army as 'barely an army, rather an episodic conglomerate of small, autonomous forces ... easy to assemble, easy to dismiss at the end of the campaign'. This description is even more apt for John's coalition, which combined English, Flemish, French and German contingents, some of whom had fought together before, some of whom were perfect strangers and viewed one another with deep suspicion.

The starting point for these 'conglomerates', the core of any medieval army, was the household (*familia*; *mesne*), the knights permanently employed by a king or great nobleman to act as his representatives, advisors and ambassadors in time of peace, and as bodyguards and soldiers in war. This could be quite a large group, by contemporary standards: King John's household contained about 100 knights at any one time. Maintaining such a force was expensive, as the lord had to feed, lodge and equip them, in addition to the regular gifts and patronage that were necessary to ensure their continued service. In return, a large household gave its lord social prestige, identifying him as a man both wealthy and generous enough to retain the service of so many men, and ensured that he always had a loyal, reliable military force at hand. The battle of Bouvines provides several examples of the courage and self-sacrifice these household knights could display in defence of their lord.

To supplement their household troops, kings and lords could call upon their vassals: people who legally owed them military service in return for

Relief from the Shrine of Charlemagne, Aachen Cathedral, completed in 1215. The emperor is in the central tent, being equipped by his servants. One (r) is tying on his chausses. Even before the invention of plate armour, the knight needed a whole team of skilled people to prepare him for battle. (INTERFOTO/Alamy Stock Photo)

land or other benefits. This 'feudal' obligation (a term mired in controversy and best avoided for our purposes) was limited, both in the number of troops the vassal was expected to supply and the length of time they could be expected to serve: 40 days was common. Depending on their wealth and status, the vassal might have a household that would fight with them or they might be a lord themselves and able to call upon their own vassals to fulfil their obligations. Obligations were not restricted to military service as a knight and could extend to the less glamorous but vital role of logistics. For example, many bishops, abbeys and towns that held land of the French king, if they did not supply actual troops, were obliged to provide a specific number of pack animals and wagons for his army.

This arrangement had significant drawbacks. Although, in theory, military service was a legal obligation, in practice the lord–vassal relationship was a good deal more reciprocal. If that relationship grew strained, a vassal might find a pretext to withhold service altogether – as exemplified by the barons of northern England flatly refusing to join King John's expedition to Poitou in 1213, saying that this was not part of their obligations to him. Even if they did answer the summons, 40 days' service was rarely enough to accomplish anything significant, particularly when campaigning in distant lands or overseas. Military service was also expensive, as individuals were required to provide their own equipment, horses and other supplies. If a leader expected to fight a prolonged campaign, it was often preferable to

David brings food to his brothers serving in Saul's army in this rare depiction of medieval military logistics in action. Note the cooking pots hanging off the sides of the wagons and the diversity of weapons and armour depicted. (Morgan MS.638 f. 27v via The Picture Art Collection/Alamy Stock Photo)

allow a vassal to commute their service to a cash payment, which could then be used to hire others in their place. In 1157, an English chronicler reported that 'every two knights equipped a third' for Henry II's Welsh campaign: this meant fewer knights but those that did serve would do so for much longer. Under the Angevin kings of England, this payment in lieu of service, known as 'scutage', could be levied at will and became, in effect, an arbitrary tax. John expanded it to include all royal tenants, not just those who owed him knight's service, and levied it 11 times in 16 years. This was one of the major complaints levelled against him by his rebel barons and continued to be a source of tension between the Crown and the English nobility for the remainder of the 13th century.

Philippe Augustus's relations with his barons were generally much better than John's and they would rally to him when summoned, but there were still limitations. Looking at the French army at Bouvines, we can see that it was composed mainly of Philippe's closest relatives, such as the de Dreux clan, and his cousin, the Duke of Burgundy, and troops from the north-eastern regions of his kingdom: Artois, Laon, Picardy, Soissons and Thiérarche, regions close to the Flanders–Hainaut border. The troops from more distant regions, particularly the Ile-de-France and the Vexin, were either with Louis in Poitou, on crusade in the south or were deliberately left behind to defend the route to Paris. It was a local army, summoned to fulfil its obligations to the king and to defend its home against the immediate threat of foreign invasion.

Both the Capetian and Angevin kings made extensive use of salaried soldiers to supplement the limited numbers they could raise through legal obligation. The terms 'salaried' or 'waged' are used here rather than 'mercenary' because the latter had a wholly negative connotation in the Middle Ages and not all paid professionals were viewed as savage freebooters. Medieval rulers relied heavily on waged soldiers but there appears to have been some sensitivity about the business of fighting for pay, especially among those who either came from the minor nobility or aspired to join it: the relationship between lord and vassal was presented as pure and virtuous, one that transcended petty concerns such as money. The economic and military realities were, of course, somewhat different. The euphemism 'stipendiaries' is common in this period, referring to knights who were retained for a wage or money-fief (land held purely for its cash value) but were not a permanent part of a household.

The lower class of waged soldier was referred to as a Brabançon (or Brabanter) or the pejorative *routier* (bandit; cut-throat). This does not mean that all soldiers of this kind came from Brabant, only that the troubled duchy of Brabant had a reputation for producing tough, effective soldiers. Kelly DeVries has even suggested

A penny of King John. Wealth in medieval Europe was measured primarily by the ownership of land and the right to tax its produce. Almost all currency took the form of silver pennies: heavy and difficult to transport in bulk but vital for paying soldiers' wages. (Robert Kawka/Alamy Stock Photo)

An army with its plunder, in the form of prisoners and livestock. 'Mercenary' soldiers had a reputation for cruelty but all medieval armies engaged in ravaging of this kind; their victims probably could not tell the difference. (BL Yates Thompson 23, f. 161 via incamerastock/Alamy Stock Photo)

A classic image of the 13th-century knight, depicted fully armed as he kneels in prayer. Note the fingerless mail 'mittens' covering his hands and the separate mail leggings. (BL Royal MS A XXII f. 220 via Photo 12/Alamy Stock Photo)

that bands of waged soldiers might have been exploiting this reputation by pretending to be from Brabant to command a higher fee. It is notable that, in England, they were collectively known as 'Flemings' (regardless of origin) and that, in 1179, when the Church condemned the use of such soldiers in the south of France, it referred to 'Brabançons, Aragonese, Navarrese, Basques, *routiers* and *Triaverdini*' (the meaning of this last is unclear but is likely similar to *routier*). Wicked mercenaries were invariably regarded as strange and foreign. The condemnation did nothing to deter the kings of Europe from employing them in large numbers: Frederick Barbarossa, Henry II and Philippe Augustus all hired them for different campaigns. The battle of

Bouvines provides one of the clearest examples of their effectiveness, when the company of 'Brabançon' foot led by Renaud, Count of Boulogne, fought with great tenacity even as the rest of the coalition army fled.

TROOPS – THE KNIGHTS (*MILITES, EQUITES*; *CHEVALIERS*)

The 13th-century knight is, arguably, the most emblematic figure of the whole European Middle Ages: rider and horse clad head-to-hoof in iron, overlayed with a brightly coloured caparison and coat of arms. While the knights were not quite the all-conquering figures depicted in contemporary poetry and romance, they were essential to all European armies. They were the military (and increasingly the social) elite and, as such, our sources tell us most about them, their equipment, their tactics and ethos.

The most important and expensive part of a knight's equipment, the thing that set him apart from the common foot soldier, was his horse. Medieval authors distinguished between different types of horse: packhorses (rounceys), riding horses (palfreys) and warhorses or chargers (destriers), and a knight would ideally possess at least one of each. The charger was the most valuable, strong enough to bear the weight of both rider and armour, trained to endure the horrors of battle and therefore ridden only in combat to preserve its stamina. We cannot say for certain how large these chargers were, given the limitations of both surviving records and archaeological evidence, but current best estimates suggest they stood between 14 and 16 hands, equivalent to a modern Arabian. By the time of Bouvines, these valuable horses were armoured like their riders, covered with mail overlaid with a cloth or silk caparison. When Guérin reported to Philippe Augustus that the coalition was pursuing the French with the intent to give battle, he told him that they were riding in formation and on 'covered horses'.

The knight himself typically wore a long coat (*hauberk*) of mail, a mesh of rivetted iron rings, that hung down to the knees and was split at the groin for ease of movement. A shirt or padded jacket (*aketon*) would be worn underneath for comfort and extra protection. Over the course of the 12th century, the hauberk's sleeves extended to cover the whole arm and the hand, with integral 'mittens' or mufflers fitted with leather palms. Separate mail leggings (*chausses*) protected the legs. The hauberk also acquired a mail hood (*coif*), with a flap of mail (*ventail*) that could be pinned or tied across the lower half of the wearer's face. It was a heavy garment, particularly around the shoulders, and wearers needed a belt to help distribute the weight. For extra protection, mail could be reinforced with pieces of shaped, boiled leather (*cuir bouilli*).

Helmets came in a variety of styles, which were probably a matter

A knight takes his fallen enemy's armour in the *Romance of Alexander*. By the early 13th century, the hauberk included a shirt, sleeves, mufflers and coif, all made as a single garment. It was, however, difficult to take on and off quickly, requiring the wearer to bend double. (The Master and Fellows of Trinity College, Cambridge, MS O.9.34 f. 17v)

A relief from the Shrine of Charlemagne. Note the curved cantle on the saddles to hold the riders in place and the loop suspending the shield around Charlemagne's neck (identified by the imperial eagle on the shield itself). (Science History Images/Alamy Stock Photo)

of individual preference. The iron cap, whether pointed, domed or flat-topped, was common, although the prominent nose guard seen on helmets on the Bayeux Tapestry seems to have declined in popularity during the 12th century. Other designs included the kettle-hat, with its wide brim, and the masked helm, which covered the wearer's face with a steel plate but left the back of his head exposed. For maximum protection, at the cost of both comfort and peripheral vision, there was the great helm (also known as the pot helm), which resembled an upturned bucket that completely enclosed the head, with a narrow eye slit and holes for ventilation. During the 13th century, the flat top of the great helm evolved into a more domed shape, which helped to deflect incoming blows.

Completing the knight's protective gear was a wooden shield, which, like the helmet, came in different shapes and sizes: contemporary illustrations show round, kite and flat-topped 'heater' shields, sometimes in the same image. It could be held on the left arm by a combination of straps or handles but, when mounted, it was hung around the neck, leaving the rider's left hand free to grip their horse's reins. The central metal boss had disappeared, creating a blank space for heraldic decorations. Warriors have painted their shields with decorative or protective symbols throughout history, of course: consider the gorgon's head of classical Greece or the Chi Ro adopted by Emperor Constantine. In 12th-century Europe these symbols took on a special significance, becoming tied to specific families, passed down between generations, and a mark of elevated social status. First appearing among the upper tiers of the aristocracy, carrying a distinctive shield (referred to as 'arms' or a 'blazon') became a sign of nobility. By the time of Bouvines, even relatively humble knightly families were adopting their own blazons, as evidenced by their tombs, seals and other material artefacts. These arms were then replicated on the sleeveless robe now worn over their mail armour (later called surcoats, hence a 'coat of arms') and their horses' caparisons. As can be imagined, this soon became very complicated, with hundreds of individual coats of arms in every kingdom. A specialist profession, the heralds, arose over the course of the 13th century, who were responsible for memorizing and eventually recording the different arms, hence the name given to the system itself: heraldry.

Heraldry in the early 13th century had not yet acquired the byzantine system of rules that would arise in later centuries but it did have a set of well-defined customs. Colours (tinctures) were restricted to bright primaries: red, blue and black were most common, as well as the so-called metals, silver and gold (white and yellow), and furs, vair (due its resemblance to squirrel fur) and ermine. There was even an element of colour theory that prohibited the placing of a colour on another colour or a metal on a metal, which made the design clear even from a distance (this applies to many modern logos too: consider the gold arches on a red field or the black horse on a gold field). The geometric divisions of the shield, such as quarters or stripes (called ordinaries), were also standardized, as were the major symbols (charges). Lions and crosses were common but there was also an element of playfulness: some nobles adopted coats of arms that punned on their names. Henri, Count of Bar, for example, whose seat was at modern Bar-le-Duc in eastern France and who fought in Philippe II's household at Bouvines, bore a shield decorated with two gold barbels.

The seal of Thibaut II, Count of Bar, son of Henri, displaying the family's arms. Its technical description is: *azure a semi of crosses fitchy or, two barbels or* (two gold barbels on a blue field covered in small gold crosses). (SC/D/797/ter Archives Nationales, France)

The principal weapon of the mounted knight was the lance: a long spear with a narrow, pointed iron tip that the rider gripped (couched) under his right arm. Used properly, with the full weight and momentum of a charging horse behind it, the lance could be thrust into an opponent, causing horrific wounds. Swords were secondary weapons, to be drawn when the lance broke or there was insufficient room to charge. Surviving examples of swords from this period are light (around 1.5kg), 76–83cm long and designed for cutting, with relatively rounded points. References to other close combat weapons, such as maces or axes, are rare and their use is less well documented. In his account of Bouvines, the English chronicler Roger of Wendover depicts Otto IV using an unusual single-edged, two-handed sword (possibly a faussard) on horseback: 'whosoever he touched he either stunned or knocked to the ground together with their horse'. Wendover was writing at both a geographical and temporal distance from the battle, however, and key parts of his account are contradicted by more immediate witnesses, so we cannot be sure about his accuracy on this point.

Guillaume le Breton reports that the coalition employed a new weapon at Bouvines, previously unknown to the French: 'long daggers, thin, three-sided, with a sharp cutting edge from the point all the way to the handle,

This striking battle scene agrees with Guillaume le Breton's description of the fighting at Bouvines. After the initial charge, the knights hacked about them with their sidearms or even wrestled with one another, stabbing at the eye slits in helms or the joints in armour with daggers. (Morgan MS M.638 f. 29v via Jimlop collection/Alamy Stock Photo)

which they used instead of swords'. These daggers were used to thrust into the eye slit of an opponent's great helm or into the joints of their hauberks. It is unlikely that they were wholly new in 1214 (although they may have been new to Guillaume). The crusader Robert de Clari reports that crusading knights used similar daggers when ambushed on a narrow forest path in 1203, where there was no room to use their lances. Regardless of when they first appeared, they represent a step in an ongoing arms race: a full suit of mail made its wearer almost impervious to conventional cutting weapons, whereas a smaller, thrusting weapon could target the weak spots in the armour.

Knights were ideally suited to the fast, fluid warfare practised in the High Middle Ages: wars of raid and counter-raid, swift strikes and sudden retreats. Noblemen were trained from a young age to ride and fight, often in the household of a friend or relative. Over the course of the 12th century, the military training exercises of these young knights evolved into a defined sport: the tournament. These were not the elegant jousts of later centuries but mock battles in which two large teams roved across the countryside, attempting to capture opponents for ransom and win renown for their skill at arms. Socially disruptive and highly dangerous, they created a sense of camaraderie and class identity among the knighthood of Western Europe.

The skills learned in the tournament were also applied on the rare occasion that participants were called upon to fight a pitched battle. The knights formed into a small troop (*cuneus*; *conroi*), each under its own banner. A group of these troops made up a battalion (*bataille*), with an army usually deploying in three battalions: left, centre and right, sometimes with a fourth held in reserve. Contemporary narratives consistently emphasize the importance of maintaining a close-packed formation and coherency between the different troops in the battalion. A chronicler of the Third Crusade described crusading knights advancing to battle: 'The vanguard of the host was wide and strong / And could well sustain fierce attacks… It was not possible to throw a prune / Except on mailed and armoured men'. Ideally, these tightly grouped knights would charge the enemy as a single body, forming an irresistible mass of iron and horseflesh that would scatter the enemy, then wheel round and charge again. Needless to say, this was a difficult manoeuvre and not always carried out successfully. At Bouvines, multiple sources describe the attack of the coalition's left wing, led by Count Fernando and his Flemish knights, as disjointed, far less effective than their opponents' effort, which was carefully arranged by the experienced Guérin.

TROOPS – THE MOUNTED SERJEANTS (*SERVIENTES, SATELLITES*; *SERGANTS À CHEVAL*)

As we turn away from the knights, our knowledge rapidly diminishes. Chronicles, poetry, manuscript illuminations and sculpture: all of these were commissioned by and for the nobility, and so reflect them and their worldview. Yet knights formed only a small proportion of contemporary armies. Our best estimates suggest that foot soldiers outnumbered knights in the French army at Bouvines at a rate of five to one, yet we know comparatively little about where they came from or how they contributed to the battle. The same is true for the mounted serjeants; we must rely on glimpses provided by the narrative histories and financial records for what little we do know.

Manuscripts of this period rarely, if ever, portray non-knightly soldiers. Even Muslims are depicted using Western arms and armour, as in this miniature of a crusading battle. Serjeants, whether mounted or on foot, were usually ignored by artists. (Acquired by Henry Walters 1903, The Walters Art Museum, MS W.137 f. 29r)

The term 'serjeant' had various meanings but, in a military context, referred to a soldier of lower status than a knight, usually a foot soldier. They should not be confused with squires (*armigeri, scutiferi*) who, in this period, were exclusively servants or valets to the nobility and were not expected to fight. A mounted serjeant occupied a position, both social and military, between foot soldier and knight: sufficiently wealthy to own and have been trained to ride a horse but still not considered a member of the elite. We get an indication of their status from Geoffroi Villehardouin's description of how the booty was divided following the sack of Constantinople in 1204. A mounted serjeant's portion was equal to two foot serjeants' portions, but half that allotted to a knight. The daily wage for a mounted serjeant in the French royal service varied across the period but, on average, he could expect between 2 sous 8 deniers and 5 sous a day, whereas a knight's pay was 6 or 7 sous.

Given their relatively humble background (probably the sons of very minor landowners) and lower wages, the mounted sergeants could not afford the full equipment necessary to fight as a knight. They are surely to be identified with the 'lightly armed horsemen' (*levis armature equites*) who fought in the French rearguard at Bouvines under Adam, Viscount of Melun, although we can only conjecture what the chronicler meant by 'lightly armed'. Presumably, they fought with less than the full suit of mail armour, leaving their legs, arms or horses undefended. They cannot have been totally unprotected, as a troop of 150 mounted serjeants from Champagne were confident enough to make the first charge of the battle proper, attacking the Flemish knights on the coalition's left wing. They appear to have operated as a kind of light cavalry, acting as scouts and raiders and supporting the knights in pitched battle.

TROOPS – THE FOOT SOLDIERS (*PEDITES*)

If we know little about the mounted serjeant, we know almost nothing about the common foot soldier in this period. They were far from helpless on the battlefield and could even discomfort the supposedly invincible knights, as they did twice at Bouvines, but the fact remains that they were regarded as auxiliary troops, rarely credited in narrative histories or depicted in visual media.

There were two distinct types of foot soldier in the High Middle Ages: the militia and the professionals. The former were organized by the larger towns, known as communes (a legal status granted by the Crown in France or declared by the more independent urban centres of the Low Countries), that were obliged to provide troops for their ruler in time of war. Philippe Augustus actively established new communes on the borders of his kingdom, particularly in the Vexin and Artois, and made them responsible for erecting new fortifications and arming their citizens for self-defence. For instance, the charter confirming the commune of Tournai, given in 1211, required the city to send 300 men to the royal army when summoned. As mentioned, the professionals were waged soldiers for whom warfare was their main or only source of income. They were likely to be more disciplined and reliable than the part-time militia and possessed vital skills, such as the use of crossbows, undermining walls or operating siege engines.

In regard to equipment, given that even members of a communal militia were expected to purchase and maintain their own equipment according to their means, there must have been great variation even within a single company. When Henry II of England issued his Assize of Arms in 1181, he mandated the military equipment that all freemen should bring with them when summoned to join the royal army. Those of the lowest tier, including all burgesses (town dwellers) and men who owned less than 10 marks in goods or chattels, were expected to own only a padded jacket (*gambeson*), an iron cap and a spear. This conforms to the depiction of foot soldiers in contemporary manuscript illuminations as lightly armoured and armed with some kind of spear or pole arm designed to cut, thrust or grab an opponent. At Bouvines, Philippe Augustus was unhorsed by foot soldiers using 'hooks and slender lances', while Renaud de Dammartin's Brabançons employed spears of such length that the French knights could not reach them with their swords.

Crossbowmen were a highly paid and highly regarded type of foot soldier, especially in siege warfare, but there are almost no references to the use of crossbows or other missile weapons at Bouvines. Guillaume le Breton describes crossbows being employed in the skirmishing between the French rearguard and the coalition on the morning of 27 July, but he does not mention them in his account of the actual battle. The so-called Anonymous of Béthune, another contemporary chronicler, makes a passing reference to a Flemish nobleman beginning the battle by charging the French crossbowmen and putting them to flight but, like Guillaume, makes no further reference to missile weapons of any kind. We must assume that either they were too few to have had any significant impact on the fighting or that the chroniclers tactfully ignored their contributions in order to emphasize the importance and valour of the knights.

Foot soldiers made up the majority of most medieval armies but we have limited evidence of their role in pitched battles. We are still a century away from the victories of Bannockburn and Courtrai, when armies dominated by common-born militia would defy the best of Europe's knighthood. Whether out of cultural prejudice on the part of their aristocratic commanders, or the limited discipline and resolve that came from being part-time soldiers, foot soldiers usually performed an auxiliary role. They were rarely called upon to advance against highly mobile knights and were most effective as large, static formations that used massed spear points and missiles to deter enemy cavalry, providing a shelter behind which friendly cavalry could rest between charges. A common tactic was to reinforce their position with wagons from the baggage train, creating a kind of defensible *laager*. The English chronicler Roger of Wendover claims the French did this at Bouvines. This is contradicted by more reliable sources but nevertheless demonstrates how contemporaries thought foot soldiers would normally fight.

The figures on the left with the prisoner are probably too well-armoured to accurately represent foot soldiers of this period (note the mail leggings), but the cluster of weapons above them indicates the variety of arms that medieval foot soldiers might carry. (Reproduced by the kind permission of the Syndics of Cambridge University Library, MS Ee.3.59 f. 5v)

The faithful defend themselves against the dragon (bottom right panel) with an array of 13th-century weapons in this illustration from the Book of Revelation. Clockwise from the top: spear, fletched javelin or dart, crossbow, axe, sword and bow. (The Master and Fellows of Trinity College, Cambridge, MS. R.16.2 f. 14r)

THE FACE OF MEDIEVAL BATTLE

A medieval battle was a nightmarish experience (what battle is not?), with hundreds or thousands of men hacking and stabbing at one another at close quarters, the wounded screaming, horses trampling on the fallen. What motivated people to enter such a terrible environment, to overcome their fear? For many, it was simple material gain: they were professionals, who earned their living by fighting. Moreover, there were many opportunities to enrich oneself: plunder was a feature of war, not an aberration, and a defeated army might abandon a fortune in its baggage train as it fled. There was also loyalty, the powerful social and political bonds that could form between a lord and his vassals, or the timeless loyalty of the soldier to the man standing beside him.

For the nobility, there were also powerful cultural forces motivating them to fight. The medieval nobility were firstly a warrior aristocracy, who justified their pre-eminent position in the social order by their willingness to risk their lives to defend their vassals and the Church against aggressors.

Noblemen were trained to fight from a very young age, raised to value courage and skills at arms and to avoid public shame at any cost. In their leisure hours, they were entertained by epic poems and the newly developed genre of romance, which mixed erotic and supernatural themes with scenes of bloody violence. This helps to explain why medieval nobility sometimes behaved in ways that ran counter to modern ideas of military logic or self-preservation. Social and cultural pressure could compel them to act against their better judgement because the stigma of cowardice or treachery that would attach itself to them and their family was considered literally worse than death.

The desire to win fame and glory was a key motivation for the knights. It is arguably why the European nobility developed the system of heraldry. It was not very useful for distinguishing friend from foe, especially in the chaos of battle. Medieval armies were much more likely to use temporary field signs: at Bouvines, the coalition wore crosses on their chests and backs for this purpose. A coat of arms was an announcement of one's individual identity: it marked the wearer as a man of status and wealth, a target worth capturing. For several centuries, custom had dictated that a knight who surrendered could expect to be captured alive and unharmed and that his captor could expect him to pay a ransom for his release. Taking a particularly wealthy prisoner in battle could make a poor knight's fortune. By wearing a coat of arms, the nobleman made himself a conspicuous target and earned honour as a man of courage.

It should be noted that this restraint did not extend to the poorer, common-born soldiers. They could not afford to pay a substantial ransom and were therefore likely to be killed out of hand. Chroniclers of this period, when they noted the numbers killed or captured in a battle, rarely mention the foot soldiers. They literally did not count. This might explain the lack of resolve among foot soldiers in this period, who knew that they could expect no mercy if they were defeated, or the desperate last stand of the Brabançons at Bouvines, unable to either surrender or escape the victorious French.

The seal of Robert Fitzwalter, one of the English barons who rebelled against John in 1215. His coat of arms is displayed on both his shield and his horse's caparison. The other shield (r) is that of Saer de Quincy, Robert's long-time friend and companion-in-arms. (Timewatch Images/Alamy Stock Photo)

ORDERS OF BATTLE

It is impossible to produce a completely accurate account of the numbers or participants involved in any 13th-century battle: we simply do not have the necessary sources and medieval chroniclers are notorious for inflating numbers for dramatic effect. Bouvines is something of an exception, however, thanks to the unusually detailed narrative accounts and surviving documentation from the French royal court. Jan F. Verbruggen used the

Servitia Feodorum, listing the royal vassals north of the Seine and the contingents they were expected to send to the royal army in 1211–12, and the *Catalogus Captivorum*, a list of the prisoners taken at Bouvines and the towns responsible for holding them, to create a plausible estimate of the numbers in the French army, which is reproduced below.

THE COALITION

Given the disparate origins of the coalition and the ad hoc nature of its army, no reliable documentation has survived to make a similar estimate for their army. It must have been as large, or even a little larger, than the French army or they would not have risked a battle on 27 July. The following is a list of key individuals named in the narrative sources or the *Catalogus Captivorum* as fighting for the coalition at Bouvines.

Otto IV, Emperor of Rome
Konrad, Count of Dortmund
Fernando, Count of Flanders
Hendrik, Duke of Brabant
Hendrik III, Duke of Limburg
Otto II, Count of Tecklenburg
Raugrafen Konrad II
Renaud, Count of Boulogne
Waleran, Count of Luxembourg
William Longespée, Earl of Salisbury

Arnoul d'Audenarde
Arnoul de Gavre
Balduin von Bergen
Baudouin de Praet
Bernhard von Horstmar
Buridan de Furnes
Dietrich von Ascheberg
Eberhard von Hisce
Eustace de Machelen
Gautier de Ghistelle

Gerhart von Moers
Gerhart von Randerath
Heinrich von Artlinburg
Heinrich von Dyck
Heinrich Rufus
Hellins de Wavrin
Hugues de Boves
Johann von Hodenberg
Lambert von Moringen
Otto von Horstmar
Paridam von Knesebeck
Philippe de Gavre
Rasse de Gavre
Rasse, son of Rasse de Gavre
Richard von Köln
Rutger von Westfalen
Simon von Saffenberg
Stephan Dessentes
Tibald von Dortmund
Wilhelm von Oberg
Wilhelm von Uetze

THE FRENCH ARMY

The numbers are the estimated number of knights that these noblemen were expected to contribute to the royal army.

Right Wing

Eudes III, Duke of Burgundy	180	Hugues de Malaunay	5
Jean, Count of Beaumont	20	Hugues de Mareuil	5
Gautier de Châtillon, Count of Saint-Pol	30	Jean de Mareuil	5
Guillaume, Count of Sancerre	10	Gilles d'Aci	5
Adam, Viscount of Melun	25	Michel d'Aci	5
Mathieu de Montmorency	20	Other knights from Champagne	180

Centre

Henri, Count of Bar	30	Guillaume de Garlande	20
Bathélemy de Roye	5	Guillaume de Montemer	5
Etienne de Longchamp	180	Jean de Rouvrai	10
Galon de Montigny	5	Pierre Tristan	5
Gautier de Nemours	5		
Gérard la Truie	5		
Guillaume des Barres	5		

Left Wing

Guillaume, Count of Ponthieu	60	Jean de Coudun	5
Pierre, Count of Auxerre, Nevers and Namur	30	Jean de Nesle	40
Robert, Count of Dreux	40	Pierre de la Tournelle	5
Philippe, Bishop of Beauvais	20	Quenon de Coudun	5
Robert, Bishop-elect of Laon	10	Thomas de Saint-Valéry	20
Gautier de Fontaines	5	Other knights from Vimeu	30
Hugues de Fontaines	5		

Position Unknown

Count of Guines	20	Raoul Flamens	5
Raoul, Count of Soissons	30	Roger de Rozoy	10
Enguerrand de Couci	30	Thomas de Mongumbert	10
Giles de Marque	5	Other knights from Amiens	20
Guy de la Roche	10		

Communal foot soldiers

Centre

Amiens	250	Compiègne	200
Arras	1,000	Corbie	200
Beauvais	500		

Location Unknown

Bruyères	120	Montreuil-sur-Mer	50
Cerny and Crépy-en-Laonnais	80	Noyon	150
Crandelain	40	Roye	100
Hesdin	80	Soissons	160
Montdidier	80	Vailly	50

To these, Verbruggen added the 150 mounted serjeants on the French right wing and the foot soldiers sent by the abbeys and smaller towns that had not been granted the status of 'commune', which he estimated at 4,000–5,000 men. This gives a total strength of about 1,200 knights and 5,000–6,000 foot. This seems quite plausible, as we know that Philippe assembled over 2,000 knights for a campaign into Poitou in September 1214. Guillaume le Breton reports that Louis was given 800 knights from the royal host to oppose John in April 1214, which would leave Philippe with around 1,200 at Bouvines.

The western facade of Cathédrale Notre-Dame d'Amiens, as it would have appeared in the 13th century. The wealthy commune of Amiens was able to send 250 men to fight at Bouvines. (Prisma by Dukas Presseagentur GmbH/Alamy Stock Photo)

THE CAMPAIGN

THE SOUTHERN CAMPAIGN – POITOU AND ROCHE-AUX-MOINES

King John landed at La Rochelle on 16 February 1214. Only two English barons accompanied him, Ranulf, Earl of Chester, and William de Ferrers, Earl of Derby, but the chronicler Ralph of Coggeshall claims John had with him 'an infinite multitude of knights of lesser wealth'. It was certainly an effective force, which was further strengthened by the local barons who declared their support for John as he advanced through the region.

John's first move was to lay siege to the castle of Milécu, a few miles south-east of La Rochelle, which surrendered in just three days. From then until mid-May, his movements are unclear but, based on the legal documents he issued and letters he sent, we know that he travelled further east and south, visiting Angoulême, Aix, Limoges and even La Reole in Gascony. His southern flank secure, he turned his attention to subduing the county

An army disembarking from its transports. Fleets of this period were made up of a mixture of manoeuvrable, oar-driven galleys and capacious sailing ships, called cogs, refitted as transports or fighting platforms. (Cambridge University Library MS Ee.3.59 f. 32v via The Picture Art Collection/Alamy Stock Photo)

The southern campaign, February–July 1214

John conducts three forays from his base at La Rochelle between 16 February and mid-May:
1. To Milécu and then Niort
2. To the western borders of Berry via Angoulême and then returning via Limoges
3. To La Reole in Gascony

4. In May, he advances into northern Poitou, taking the castles of Miervant and Vouvant
5. Having divided the royal army with his father at Châteauroux the previous month, Louis moves west to attack the castle at Moncontour
6. John moves east to threaten Louis, who withdraws north to Chinon
7. John receives the homage of the Poitevin barons at Parthenay, then advances north to Ancenis in eastern Brittany
8. 13 June: John advances west to neutralize the garrison at Nantes and receives the surrender of Angers itself on 17 June
9. 19 June: John moves to besiege the castle at Roche-aux-Moines
10. Louis advances west to attack John, arriving on 2 July

of Poitou and the powerful Lusignan family in particular. On 17 May, John took the Lusignans' castle at Miervant by assault and two days later laid siege to Geoffroi de Lusignan himself at Vouvant. In a letter, sent to England to report his progress and preserved in the chronicle of Roger of Wendover, John describes how he bombarded the castle continuously for three days with his 'stone throwers' (*petrarii*) until Geoffroi surrendered.

Philippe was well aware that John had landed but it is difficult to recreate his precise movements in early 1214. Guillaume le Breton tells us that Philippe came south from Paris, having stationed garrisons on the borders of Vermandois and Boulogne, and ravaged the lands of those barons who had submitted to John, specifically naming Thouars, Chollet, Bressuire and Vielle. In April, at Châteauroux, Philippe made the decision to divide his army, leaving his heir Louis and Henri Clément, Marshal

An army attacks a stronghold by escalade. John did not have to resort to such desperate and dangerous methods to take the castles of Poitou: a few days' bombardment by his stone throwers was enough to convince them to surrender. (Acquired by Henry Walters 1903, The Walters Art Museum, MS W.137 f. 235r)

The 15th-century Château des ducs de Bretagne, Nantes. As a strategic port on the Loire with access to the Bay of Biscay, Nantes was first fortified in the 3rd century CE and would remain a focus for military activity for centuries. (Photo by Andia/Universal Images Group via Getty Images)

of France, with some 800 knights to continue the war in Poitou while he himself returned north to meet the rest of John's coalition.

According to John, while he was at Vouvant he heard that Louis was besieging the castle at Moncontour, so marched east to attack him. Louis withdrew to Chinon. On 25 May, John was at Parthenay, where he received the homage of Geoffroi de Lusignan, Raoul d'Issoudun, Count of Eu, and Aimery de Lusignan, Count of La Marche, betrothing his infant daughter Isabella to the latter's son to secure their allegiance. From there, his next target was Nantes, on Brittany's south-west coast, which he besieged in early June. He could not afford to leave the city's garrison unchecked, as it might harass his supply lines as he moved north into Anjou. Philippe knew the importance of Nantes and had given command of the garrison to Robert III de Dreux. While Robert could be trusted not to betray the city, the young commander proved too rash. Rather than withstand a siege and wait for Louis to relieve him, Robert sallied out to deny John the bridges that controlled the approach to the city. John withdrew and Robert, pursuing, was captured along with 20 of his knights by ambush parties hidden in the bushes. With Nantes suitably neutered, John turned east and north to Angers, his family's ancestral seat. The city walls had been demolished following Philippe's conquests in 1204 and the citizens surrendered without resistance on 17 June.

John likely intended to use Angers as a base for campaigning into Maine or beyond. To secure his line of supply, however, John first needed to take the castle of Roche-aux-Moines. Recently built by Guillaume des Roches, Philippe's seneschal of Anjou, on a cliff overlooking the Loire, the castle controlled all traffic, by river and road, between Nantes and Angers. John began the siege on 19 June, probably expecting a repeat of his earlier, swift victories. He was to be disappointed.

The garrison of Roche-aux-Moines, commanded by Guillaume des Roches himself, proved unusually stubborn, holding out for over two weeks despite the ongoing bombardment from John's siege engines. Guillaume le Breton describes how the garrison shot at the besiegers with 'darts and arrows, threw planks and bits of timber', even tearing down the roofs of buildings to make more ammunition. He also recorded an incident during the siege that he called an 'admirable new trick'. One of the besiegers, a hardened robber named Enguerrand Brisemoutier (which means 'monastery-

A siege from the 14th-century *Codex Manesse*. Crossbowmen shoot at the defenders while others assault the gate, attempting to either burn it or break it down with axes. The defenders respond with crossbow bolts and stones. Note the lady (centre) aiding in the defence, poised to throw a stone. (Pictorial Press Ltd/ Alamy Stock Photo)

THE DEATH OF ENGUERRAND BRISEMOUTIER AT ROCHE-AUX-MOINES, JUNE 1214 (PP.46–47)

The death of Enguerrand Brisemoutier ('monastery-breaker') at the siege of Roche-aux-Moines, based on the account of Guillaume le Breton. Enguerrand, a 'violent brigand' from Poitou, is presented here in full armour, including mail leggings **(1)**. During the siege he had taken to approaching the castle walls under the cover of a large shield held by a servant **(2)** and sniping at the defenders with a crossbow. The crossbow was a fearsome weapon, capable of penetrating mail armour, and the aristocracy were quite willing to use it in battle. Philippe Augustus shot at the defenders of Acre with a crossbow in 1191 and Richard the Lionheart carried one when he stormed the beaches near Jaffa in 1192.

A member of the garrison **(3)** devised an ingenious method to circumvent Enguerrand's defences. He tied a thin rope to a post on the wall and attached the other end to a crossbow bolt. When Enguerrand approached the walls, he shot the bolt into the shield and pulled on the rope, causing both shield and servant to fall into the castle moat **(4)**. This left Enguerrand exposed to the castle walls and he was duly shot by the other defenders **(5)**. Crossbowmen were usually professional soldiers, well-paid and valued for their skills. Royal castles in both France and England were supplied with dozens of crossbows and thousands of bolts: in March 1261, King John's heir, Henry III, ordered the constable of St Briavels castle to send 10,000 crossbow bolts to Marlborough.

A 14th-century illumination depicting John's southern campaign. (L) John and his army fight the garrison of Nantes. (R) Louis leads his army to relieve Roche-aux-Moines. (BL Royal 16 G VI f. 385 via World History Archive/Alamy Stock Photo)

breaker', almost certainly a nickname), was in the habit of walking before the castle walls and sniping at the garrison with a crossbow, all the while protected by a large shield, which was carried in front of him by a servant. According to Guillaume, a member of the garrison contrived to tie one end of a fine cord to a crossbow bolt and the other to a post on the battlement. He then shot the bolt into Enguerrand's shield, hauled on the rope and pulled both shield and servant into the nearby moat. Enguerrand, now exposed, was immediately shot and killed by the garrison. John was reportedly so angry about this that he had a gallows erected in sight of the castle walls, threatening to hang the entire garrison if they did not surrender at once, but to no effect.

On 2 July, John learned that Louis's army was within a day's march of Roche-aux-Moines. Guillaume le Breton claims Louis sent a message to John, challenging him to meet him in a pitched battle. John answered: 'If you come, you will find us ready to fight; the sooner you come, the sooner you will regret it'. Whether this really happened, or is simply poetic licence, all our contemporary sources agree that John was willing to fight. Unfortunately for him, his Poitevin barons were not. They had been content to do homage to John and support him while he was on hand with an army but they clearly did not believe that he would be able to protect them from the consequences of fighting their future king. Once again, John's political and diplomatic weakness undermined his military ambitions. Unable to persuade his supposed vassals to fight, John fled, abandoning much of his baggage and siege equipment for Louis to plunder.

Just two days later, John was at Pouzauges, over 60 miles south of Roche-aux-Moines, and by 9 July he was back at La Rochelle, where he sent another letter to England, begging his barons to send reinforcements without delay. Louis let him be, content to punish the local lords who had supported John by plundering their lands and reclaiming the castles John had taken in the spring. The southern campaign was an almost total failure, save for one thing – it had forced Philippe and Louis to divide their army. There was still every chance that Otto, and the other members of John's coalition, might win a decisive victory.

The northern campaign, 12–26 July 1214

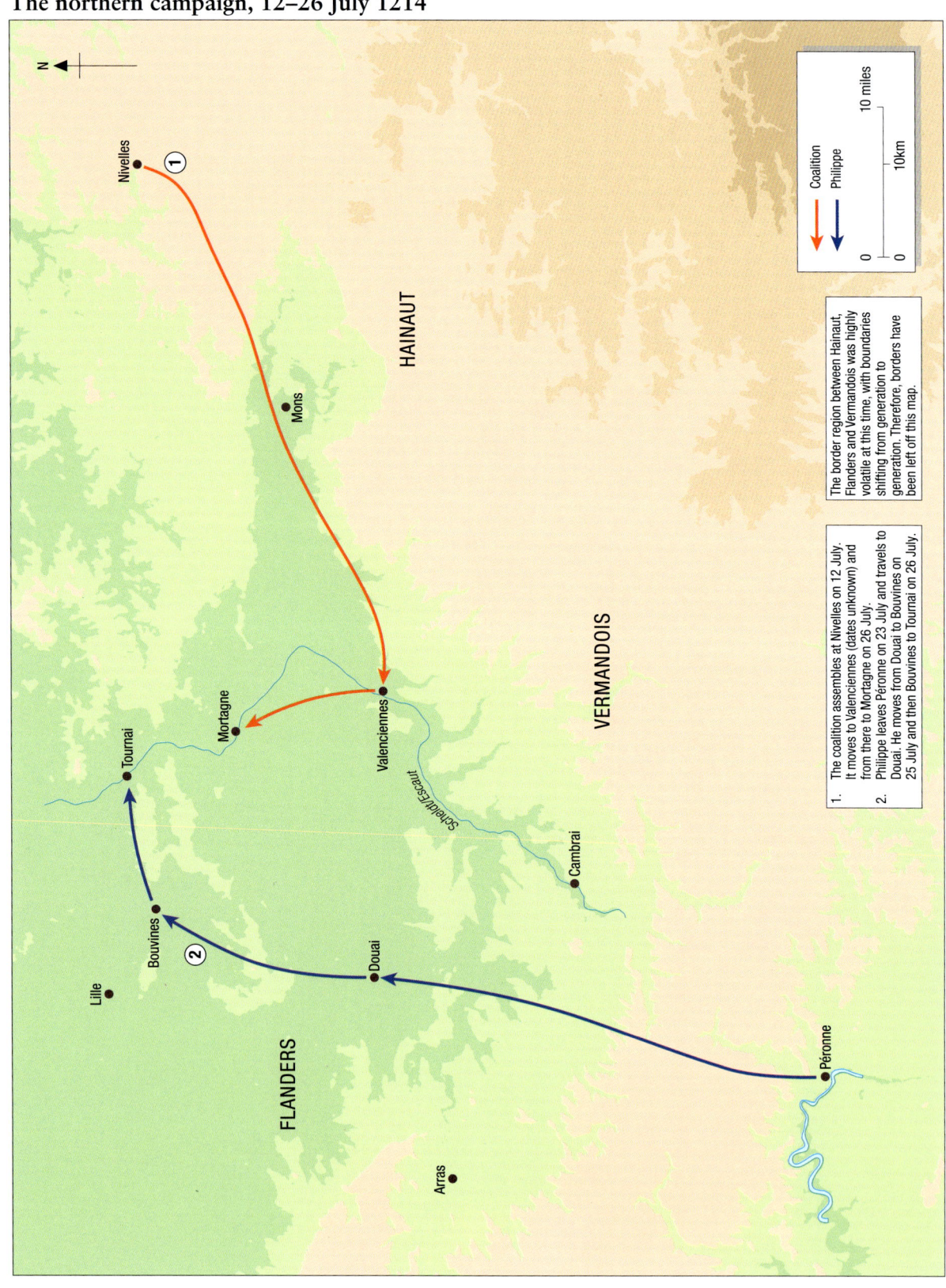

50

Valenciennes town hall, built in the 19th century. Almost nothing survives of the medieval town: the Hindenburg Line ran through the town during World War I and it was the scene of heavy fighting again in 1944. (Hemis/Alamy Stock Photo)

THE NORTHERN CAMPAIGN – THE ROAD TO BOUVINES

The coalition army – Emperor Otto, Count Fernando, Count Renaud and the rest of John's allies – assembled at Nivelles in southern Brabant on 12 July. From there, they marched south and west, into Hainaut, to the town of Valenciennes. Philippe mustered his army (less the troops he had left with Louis at Châteauroux) at Péronne on the River Somme. On 23 July, he marched north, out of French royal territory and into Flanders. He crossed the Scarpe at Douai, then continued north and east, marching parallel to the frontier with Hainaut, crossing the Marcq at the village of Bouvines on 25 July and reaching the city of Tournai on 26 July. Guillaume le Breton proudly describes how his master ravaged Fernando's lands as he went, 'pillaging and devastating everything on his right and left with fire in a royal manner'. The coalition had been raiding likewise into the prince-bishopric of Cambrai, while the majority of the army marched north to the castle at Mortagne. It seems that each was unaware of the other's location, as the two armies had managed to march past one another: in an age when armies were small, communication relied largely on word of mouth and maps were symbolic rather than scientific, it was difficult to acquire recent, accurate intelligence. This is how, on 26 July 1214, Philippe learned the enemy was actually 10 miles south of his position, threatening his line of retreat.

Notre-Dame Cathedral, Tournai, much as it would have appeared to Philippe and his army in 1214. Built at the start of the 12th century, it is an early example of the Gothic style that characterized church architecture in the High Middle Ages. (Santiago Urquijo via Getty Images)

Hendrik of Brabant's seal. The duke is depicted as a mounted knight with a flat-topped helmet, holding a lance with a pennant and a shield bearing his arms: *sable a lion rampant or* (a gold lion on a black field). (21607 Archives de l'État en Belgique)

According to Guillaume le Breton, who was Philippe's chaplain and with him throughout the Bouvines campaign, it was Hendrik, Duke of Brabant, who informed the king of the coalition's location. Hendrik was Philippe's son-in-law and had been compelled to join the coalition because Fernando held his sons hostage. He was evidently trying to play both sides in the hope that, should Philippe be victorious, he would still find favour at the Capetian court. According to Guillaume, Hendrik sent a 'certain cleric' in secret to Philippe to tell him that the coalition was at Mortagne and that the approach to the castle would be very difficult. He told him 'how the way was narrow and thick with willows, how it was a muddy swamp, how the reeds would hinder him on his way to Mortagne, how the horses and wheeled vehicles could scarcely go that way'.

Philippe called his advisors and chief noblemen together for a council of war. Guillaume le Breton's two accounts contradict one another here. In the earlier *Gesta*, he wrote that Philippe wanted to attack Mortagne and that his advisors had to dissuade him, citing the difficult terrain, suggesting instead that the army withdraw and find another route into Hainaut. When he revised his history into the later *Philippide*, Guillaume subtly changed his account: now the withdrawal was Philippe's plan all along, a ruse to draw the coalition onto more favourable ground for a pitched battle. The anonymous chronicler writing for Robert of Béthune (who fought for the coalition) interpreted the withdrawal as a simple retreat, motivated by fear of being attacked by the coalition army. Regardless of his reasoning, Philippe made the decision to begin the return journey west the next day, 27 July, via the bridge at Bouvines.

THE BATTLE – 27 JULY 1214

Reconstructing a medieval battle is a difficult exercise. Most of the sources were written by churchmen with little practical experience of war, who were rarely present at the battle itself and had to rely on witness testimonies or general gossip for their information. Bouvines is unusual in that one of the main sources, Guillaume le Breton, was actually present at the battle. He describes: 'At that moment stood behind the king, not far from him, the chaplain who wrote this and other clerics, hearing the sound of the trumpets, in a loud voice sang the psalm, "Blessed be God who teaches me", right through'. Guillaume produced two accounts of Bouvines, both in Latin. The earlier, part of the *Gesta Philippi Augusti* (*The Deeds of Philippe Augustus*), is in prose and provides the most complete narrative of the battle. The later *Philippide*, an epic poem modelled on a medieval account of Alexander the Great, is substantially similar but embellishes the narrative with eloquent speeches and topographical descriptions. Yet even an eyewitness view, like Guillaume's, could only

A monastic scribe writing on parchment (note the knife for scraping mistakes from the parchment). Most accounts of medieval battles were composed by men who had little experience of war: Guillaume le Breton is a notable exception. (The Master and Fellows of Trinity College, Cambridge, MS O.9.34 f. 22r)

Tournai to Bouvines, 27 July 1214

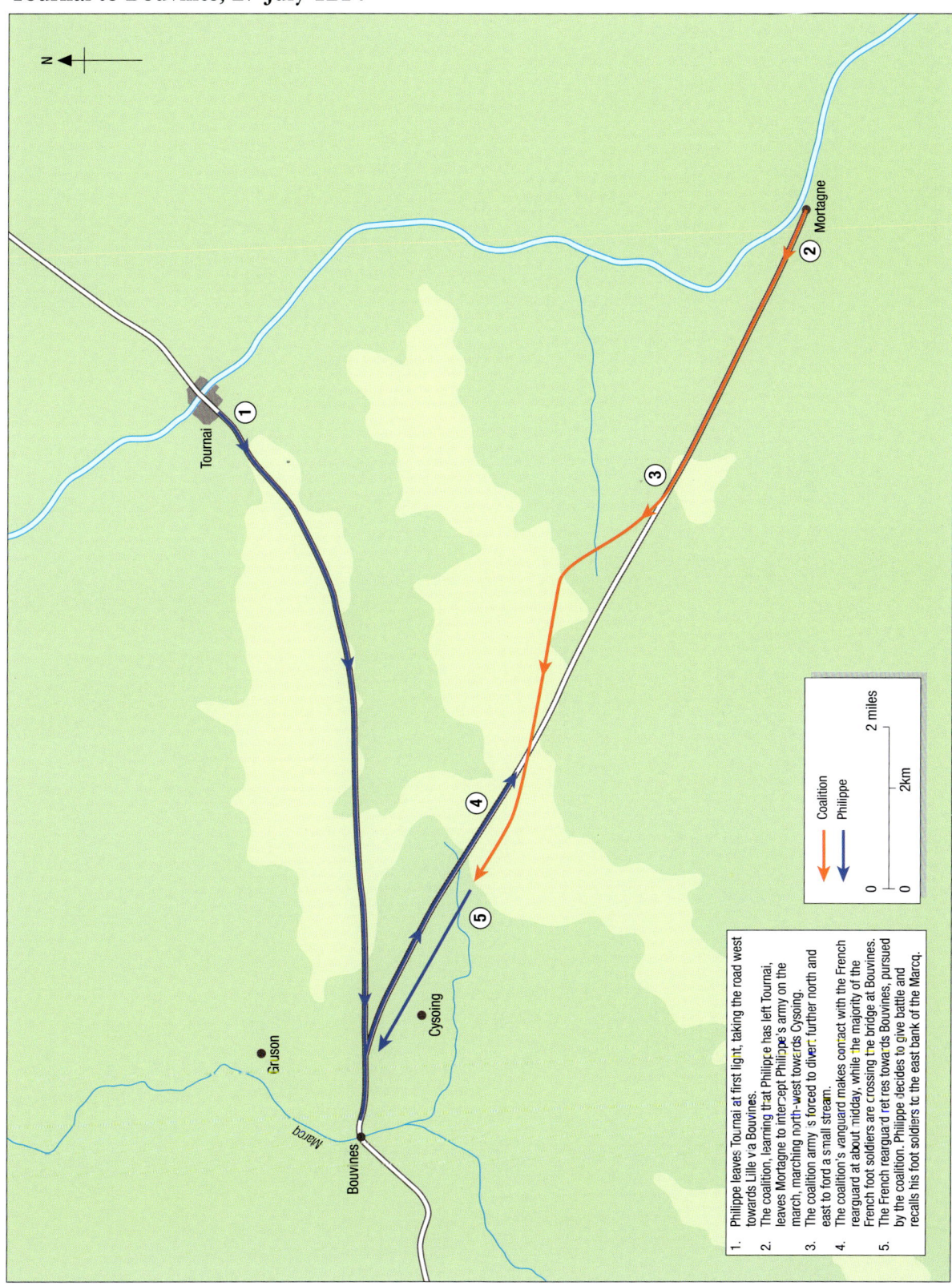

The Noble Tour in Lille, part of the fortifications constructed by Philippe II, Duke of Burgundy (r. 1363–1404) during the Hundred Years War. Philippe Augustus intended to lodge his army at Lille on 27 July but was intercepted by the coalition before he could reach it. (Frédéric Araujo/Alamy Stock Photo)

ever be limited. By his own admission, he was stationed at the rear of the French army, behind Philippe. He was not in a position to observe the whole field and, once the fighting began and the dust rose, it is unlikely that he was able to see even a fraction of what happened. It is likely that he relied on the testimony of others who had been in the French army when writing his account. These witnesses were probably in the right wing and the king's household, as these are the two areas of the battlefield that feature most prominently in his narratives. As such, there is very little known about what happened on the French left during the battle and this may have as much to do with Guillaume's sources as the actual events of 27 July 1214.

In addition to Guillaume's narratives there is also the *Chronique des rois de France* (*Chronicle of the Kings of France*), written in Old French by the so-called Anonymous of Béthune. This unknown author was closely connected to the lords of Béthune (in modern Pas-de-Calais), who feature prominently in his narrative. He may even have been a member of the household of Robert VII of Béthune, who fought for the coalition at Bouvines. The *Chronique* provides a valuable alternate perspective on the battle, one that occasionally contrasts with the clerical, royalist views of Guillaume le Breton.

Morning
Philippe left Tournai at dawn, taking the old Roman road west. His destination was Lille, a journey of about 20 miles. Guillaume le Breton claims that Philippe was reluctant to fight that day because it was a Sunday and that he was compelled to violate the holy day by his enemies. This is not implausible, as Philippe was noted for his personal piety, but he does not appear to have expected Otto to show the same restraint. The French army travelled at pace: 'they were in such haste that those who saw them swore that they had never seen so great a host ride so swiftly' (*Chronique des rois*).

When their scouts reported that Philippe was heading west, the coalition's leaders held a council to debate what they should do. All sources agree that it was a fractious meeting, with accusations of cowardice and treachery thrown back and forth and no single guiding voice to steer matters. Otto, as both a king and emperor, might have been expected to assume overall command but he did not, either because he lacked the force of personality or because he had contributed little in the way of troops or money to the campaign. John was the paymaster, giving his representatives, William, Earl of Salisbury, and the Picard renegade-turned-stipendiary Hugues de Boves, a great deal of influence.

The question before the coalition was whether to pursue Philippe and force an engagement, or allow him to withdraw unmolested. Renaud, Count of Boulogne, was against fighting. Roger of Wendover (an English chronicler sympathetic to John's cause) claims this was out of a pious respect for that day being a Sunday: '[it was] an outrage to spill human blood on such day'. This seems unlikely. Renaud probably feared that Philippe's withdrawal was a ruse, intended to draw the coalition into an ambush, or that the coalition would not be able to pursue quickly enough to catch him unprepared. With the benefit of hindsight we know that this was sound advice but the other leaders did not trust Renaud, a man well known for switching allegiances when it suited him. Hugues de Boves called Renaud 'a vile traitor', saying that he was either 'timid or lazy' and reproaching him for his ingratitude to John, who had given him many gifts and extensive lands in England. Guillaume le Breton claims that the other leaders actually threatened to imprison Renaud if he did not agree to join them in their attack on the French. Stung by the accusations, Renaud reportedly said to Hugues, 'Today you will run away scared; but I will fight in peril of my life, and stay until I am captured or killed'. Ironically, nobody appears to have suspected Hendrik of Brabant, who had actually passed intelligence to Philippe the night before.

Renaud was shouted down and the decision was taken to pursue Philippe along the Chaussée Brunehaut, another Roman road that ran north-west from Mortagne and joined the Tournai road north of the village of Cysoing. It was a narrow road that ran through dense woodland but it was the only route that would allow the coalition to catch Philippe before he reached Lille. They almost certainly did not expect to fight a pitched battle that day. It is far more likely they hoped to overtake Philippe on the march and overwhelm his rearguard while the bulk of the army was strung out along the road or crossing the bridge at Bouvines. Richard the Lionheart had accomplished something very similar at Fréteval in 1194, when he captured Philippe's baggage, including the French royal seal.

While the French army pressed on towards Lille, Guérin and Adam, Viscount of Melun, leading a small troop of mounted serjeants, withdrew to perform a reconnaissance. Travelling about 3 miles south of the road, they climbed a hill to get a better view of the surrounding country. They were surprised to see the coalition army, fully armed and arranged to fight: '[there were] knights on covered horses and serjeants on foot going before them, which was a very clear sign that there was about to be a battle'. The French observed that the coalition was heading north and east: a 'little river' cut across their road and they were obliged to turn aside to locate a suitable

An army pursues its enemies into a stronghold. It is highly unlikely that the coalition intended to fight a pitched battle at Bouvines. They believed (or hoped) something like this would happen; that they would run the French down as they fled to Lille, with minimal loss to their own forces. (The Master and Fellows of Trinity College, Cambridge, MS O.9.34 f. 12v)

Bouvines as it appears today, viewed from the west. The village skyline is dominated by the Church of St Peter, constructed in 1878. The medieval church where Philippe prayed before the battle would have been much less imposing. (Hemis/Alamy Stock Photo)

ford. Guérin, greatly alarmed, left Adam to keep a watch on the enemy while he rode back to inform Philippe of the danger.

The king ordered his army to halt and summoned his senior noblemen to discuss what should be done: a clear example of the limited, almost conciliatory, nature of royal authority in this period. Even when faced with a military emergency, Philippe needed to seek advice from his chief vassals. Nobody was certain what the coalition intended to do. Some did not believe that they would attack and argued that they were actually heading east to occupy Tournai. Others at the council, Guérin chief among them, thought that the coalition would soon resume their march north-west, that they intended to attack and that Philippe should deploy his army to defend itself. Others argued that it was too risky to give battle and that it would be safer to press on to Lille, where the army would be protected by the town's fortifications. Whether out of caution, or a mistaken belief that the coalition was indeed going to Tournai, Philippe chose to resume the march.

Bouvines was (and remains) a small village, only notable in 1214 for its church, dedicated to St Peter, and a bridge across the small but swampy River Marcq. Guillaume le Breton reports that Philippe had the bridge widened to accommodate his army 'so that twelve people could cross over side-by-side together and eight men leading their four-horse wagons'. Most of the baggage and the foot soldiers were already on the west bank when Philippe himself reached Bouvines at about noon. It was a hot day and the king took the opportunity to remove his armour and rest in the shade of an ash tree, taking a meal of bread and wine. It was here that messengers from the rear of the army found him. Their report confirmed Guérin's prediction: the enemy was not going to Tournai after all but was even now attacking the French rearguard and driving them back.

Archers attack from the trees. Ambushes of this kind were a common feature of medieval warfare, especially as soldiers rarely travelled wearing their armour, so an unexpected attack could be highly effective. (The Master and Fellows of Trinity College, Cambridge, MS O.9.34 f. 26r)

There are few details known about this action but it was arguably one of the key moments of the whole battle. The rear of a medieval army on the march was a place of distinction and honour, as it was the most likely place to be ambushed and therefore the most dangerous. In February 1250, Gautier de Châtillon (nephew of the Gautier who fought at Bouvines) begged Philippe's grandson, Louis IX, to give him command

Philippe Augustus offers to give up his crown, by Horace Vernet. This moment would remain an enduring symbol of the relationship between the French monarchy and their subjects. This painting is situated in the Gallery of Great Battles at Versailles, built by Louis Philippe I between 1833 and 1837. (Photo by Art Media/Print Collector/Getty Images)

of the crusaders' rearguard at the battle of Mansurah. On 27 July 1214, that distinction went to Eudes III, Duke of Burgundy (1166–1218). Eudes was an experienced soldier and veteran of the tournament field, who had only recently returned from crusading against heretics in southern France. Guillaume le Breton says that his force consisted of crossbowmen, under Adam of Melun, and 'lightly armed horsemen and serjeants from Champagne'. These may have been mounted crossbowmen, a documented feature of the French army in this period and distinguished from ordinary crossbowmen in the royal accounts of 1202–03. It is unclear whether they actually shot from the saddle, using lighter bows that could be drawn by hand, or if they acted as a kind of mounted infantry that could deploy, shoot and redeploy faster than conventional foot soldiers.

The coalition's attack was led by the Flemish contingent, who had crossbowmen of their own. The Anonymous of Béthune says the two sides made contact in a wood 'two leagues from Tournai' and began a running battle under the trees. The Flemings had the better of it, forcing the French to retire towards Bouvines five times. Nevertheless, through a combination of Eudes's resistance, the narrowness of the road, and the time spent finding fords to cross the 'little river', the coalition army had been unable to take Philippe by surprise. Upon hearing that the enemy had engaged his rearguard, Philippe ordered those troops who had already crossed the bridge to return to the east bank. He briefly entered St Peter's church to pray, put on his armour and sounded the call to arms.

It was at this point that one of the most famous moments of the whole battle reportedly occurred. According to an anonymous French chronicler, known only as the Minstrel of Reims, Philippe called his senior vassals to him. They shared bread and wine in a ritual very much intended to parallel the Eucharist. Then the king made an extraordinary offer:

And when the king saw this he was very happy and said to them: 'My lords, you are all my men, and I am your lord, such as I am, and I have loved you

> very much and held you in high honour and given generously to you; I have never done you any wrong or injustice but always treated you as was right. By God, I beg you all, that you guard my person and my honour and your own. And if you know of one among you who would wear the crown better than me, I will give it to him willingly, with a good heart and will'. When the barons heard him say this, they began to weep for pity and said: 'My lord, for God's sake! We want no other king but you! Why then, ride boldly against your enemies and we are prepared to die alongside you'.

This scene is almost certainly an invention, either by the Minstrel themselves or their source. Guillaume le Breton does not mention it, nor do the other earlier chroniclers. Nevertheless, it is a valuable insight into the medieval concept of good lordship and the French monarchy's public image. First, it is a personal appeal from Philippe to his vassals. There are no references to abstract values or a sense of French nationhood. He speaks instead of the relationship he has with each individual: that he has been generous to them, treating them with justice and honour. Now he asks them to reciprocate, protecting not only his physical body (*mon cors*) but, equally important, his reputation and their own (*m'oneur et la vostre*). The theatrical offer of the crown and the barons' collective refusal is also important. By acclaiming him as their king, the barons effectively elect Philippe as their leader. The event itself may be fiction but it tells us how the Capetian kings wanted to be seen. They wanted to be perceived, at least, to rule by consent: generous and just lords, receiving their due service from faithful subjects. This is a world away from absolutist notions of rule by 'divine right'. It is surely significant that the Minstrel's chronicle was composed at around the same time that the English parliament was battling with King John's son, Henry III, over the limits of royal power. The great princes of Germany were constantly at war with one another and their king: the Welf–Staufen civil war that elevated Otto IV to the imperial throne was simply one in a long line of such dynastic struggles. By comparison, France was peaceful and prosperous, its kings enjoying good relations with their subjects and victory over their enemies. The historical Philippe, of course, could not know how the events of 27 July would transpire. Pitched battles between armies of equal strength were rare for a good reason: the outcome was uncertain. As his army deployed on the plain before Bouvines, he knew that he faced either a divinely ordained victory or a defeat that would end his campaign and, perhaps, his dynasty.

Afternoon – deployment

The coalition may not have achieved total surprise but Philippe was still in a dangerous position. The majority of his army, made up of slow-moving foot soldiers, was on the western bank of the Marcq. His priority was to screen the crossing while they crossed over and deployed to fight. To this end, he sent Guérin, his most able commander, to take command of the rearguard, which he reinforced with additional knights to form a formidable cavalry force. Guérin took responsibility for deploying this battalion, as described in the *Gesta Philippi*:

> He placed some who were in the front further back, knowing them to be fearful and timid. But those who were worthy and reliable, he put them in the front of the battalion and said to them: 'The field is wide; spread yourselves

The army of the Beast from the 'Trinity Apocalypse'. Although very much an abstract representation of a battalion, this image conveys both the close formation that knights adopted in battle and the importance of banners for identification and unit cohesion. (The Master and Fellows of Trinity College, Cambridge, MS R.16.2 f. 23r)

out across the plain lest the enemy surround you. It is not fitting that one knight be made the shield of another; but remain firm so that you may all fight on one front'.

He was clearly concerned that the coalition might outflank the French, so deployed on as broad a front as possible. The *Gesta Philippi* claims the battalion was 1,040 paces wide. Assuming this is the same as the *pas ordinaire* of later medieval France (0.812m), this means its front covered approximately 2,770ft or just over 844m. Guérin's instruction that one knight should not be 'the shield of another' is an interesting insight into the psychology of the mounted knight. Presumably, the instinct for self-preservation caused individuals to hang back, or to creep gradually behind their neighbour and avoid the full shock of first contact with the enemy, thereby protecting themselves but diluting the impact of the battalion's charge.

The coalition leaders were astonished to find a French battalion deployed and ready to fight. A local chronicler claims Otto was heard to exclaim: 'Were we not told that the king was fleeing, that he was afraid to await our arrival? And lo! I see his force, a very strong force, and its divisions properly ordered and prepared for battle'. As they were not confident about attacking Guérin's large, well-ordered battalion with the limited forces in their vanguard, they were left with only two choices: to make a shameful retreat in the face of the enemy, and risk Philippe pursuing them in turn, or to commit everything by fighting a pitched battle. Whether out of pride, confidence or desperation, the coalition began to deploy on the open plain to the east of Bouvines.

It is here that historians' interpretations of the chronicle evidence diverge into two camps. John France is the main proponent of what might be called the 'meeting engagement' model of the battle. In this interpretation, Guérin's screening force attacked the coalition's left wing early in the afternoon, before the rest of the French army had fully deployed on the northern part of the field. France theorizes that Guérin wanted to take advantage of the disorder within the coalition army as it deployed from marching column to battle array. This was followed by a separate counter-attack by Otto in the centre with the forces that had managed to deploy. In this interpretation, a significant number of coalition troops never made contact with the French but retreated when they saw that their vanguard had been bested. This theory has several elements to recommend it. If we accept that the French were outnumbered at Bouvines, this would explain why the coalition's superior numbers did not affect the outcome. It explains why the chroniclers have so little to say about events on the northern side of the battle: there was relatively little fighting as the coalition was already in retreat by the time the French left wing was fully deployed. It also demonstrates sound tactical logic. All the available evidence suggests that Guérin was a bold and observant commander. It makes sense that he would press his advantage, attacking before the coalition was prepared to fight.

The alternative interpretation, based on the work of Verbruggen and others, could be called the 'set piece' model of Bouvines. According to this theory, the two armies held off engaging for a considerable length of time until they had both fully deployed on the plain east of the village. Only then did Guérin take the decision to begin hostilities by sending forward his light cavalry. This seems to be the more convincing model, as it accords more closely with the chronicle accounts. According to the *Chronique des rois*: 'when the two hosts had advanced that they could see one another plainly, both sides paused for a long time and arranged themselves'. Guillaume le Breton's description also indicates a long pause between the coalition's arrival and Guérin's attack:

> [Otto] retired a little to the right and, arranging his divisions, moved to the north. Stretching his force across a great space, he formed a line of armed men two thousand paces long. So the king also took care to stretch his wings likewise, lest he be surrounded or cut off by so many enemies... And the divisions considered one another directly, separated by a small area of the plain, face to face, nor did anybody make a sound. (*Philippide*)

This suggests a significant degree of caution, even timidity on both sides. There were probably several reasons for this. Soldiers of this period had no tradition of formal drill, let alone practising complex manoeuvres as a whole army. At Bouvines, both commanders had to bring their forces across an obstacle before they deployed: Philippe's foot had to cross back over the Marcq, while the coalition army had to debouche from the Tournai road. Orders could only be delivered by word of mouth or through very basic signals given with banners and trumpets, making it very difficult for a commander to affect the course of a battle once it had begun. This made it vital that every man was in his place and had a clear idea of what he was expected to do. Moreover, the side that advanced first, if their attack was uncoordinated, risked making itself vulnerable to a counter-attack. It was not uncommon, before and after Bouvines, for armies to deploy for battle in sight of the enemy and remain there until sunset, both commanders waiting for the other to make the first move. The chronicler Jean le Bel, who wrote an account of his service in the army of Edward II of England in 1327, described how the English and Scottish armies stood facing one another across a river for three days, neither willing to cross and fight on the enemy's ground. Medieval commanders were quite willing to attack an unprepared enemy but only at minimal risk to themselves. At Bouvines, with neither side willing or able to withdraw, the only alternative was to deploy as best as they could and trust to God and fate to decide the outcome.

The battlefield was delimited by the two marshes bordering the Marcq: the Marais de Willems in the north and the Marais de Louvil in the south. The plain itself was ideal cavalry ground: level, open and sloping gently down to the river. The coalition deployed here, north of the Tournai road, perhaps hoping to take advantage of the slight incline. This meant that they were facing west, however, and had the sun in their eyes. The French also extended their battle-line north, 'the sun on their shoulders' (*Gesta Philippi*), wary of being outflanked or even cut off from the bridge behind them. As has already been noted, the *Philippide* states the coalition's front line was 2,000 paces long (approximately 1 mile or just over 1.6km), which the French deployed to match. If we accept the description of Guérin's battalion from the *Gesta Philippi*, this means that the French 'right wing' actually made up more than half the army's battle-line. Guillaume le Breton describes Robert de Dreux's battalion (nominally the army's left wing) as 'close to the king, so that there was no space between his division and the king's', suggesting that the French army was effectively made up of two 'bodies': the cavalry force screening the bridge and the remainder, including the foot soldiers, which deployed to the north.

Philippe's nominal 'left wing' was commanded by his cousin, Robert II, Count of Dreux, whose son, Robert III, was now John's prisoner in England after being taken at Nantes the previous month. With him was his brother Philippe, Bishop of Beauvais. With the de Dreux brothers were the king's brother-in-law, Guillaume, Count of Ponthieu, commanding 'the men of Gamaches and Ponthieu' (*Philippide*), and yet another royal cousin, Pierre de Courtenai, Count of Auxerre, Nevers and Namur. Opposite them, on the coalition's right, were two of the coalition's most formidable commanders: Renaud, Count of Boulogne, and William, Earl of Salisbury.

Otto took up position in the centre of his army, 'in the middle of a close-packed formation' (*Gesta Philippi*), where he erected his standard:

> He mounted a pole on a wagon [and] attached a dragon to the pole, so that it could be seen at a distance. It drank the winds and its tail and wings swelled up, its teeth bristled and its maw gaped wide. The wings of Jupiter's golden eagle overhung it all; its whole surface shone with gold, imitating the sun. (*Philippide*)

Otto IV's coat of arms. An example of 'dimidation', displaying half of two different coats of arms side-by-side: in this case, the Angevin leopards and the imperial eagle. This practice would be supplanted by 'impalement', in which both coats are displayed in full, one in each half of the shield. (British Library Royal MS 14 C VII f. 86v)

From this description we can infer that the 'dragon' (*draco*) was a kind of windsock, perhaps an imitation of the king of England's traditional 'dragon banner', while the eagle was an ancient symbol of the Roman empire. Like his personal coat of arms, which placed the Angevin leopards alongside the imperial eagle, Otto's standard proclaimed his dual Anglo-German heritage. Mounting a standard of this kind on a wagon, where it could be easily seen and act as a rallying point for the army, was not uncommon. They are usually associated with medieval Italy, where they were called *carroccio*: objects of great civic pride, adorned with sacred images, which accompanied a city's

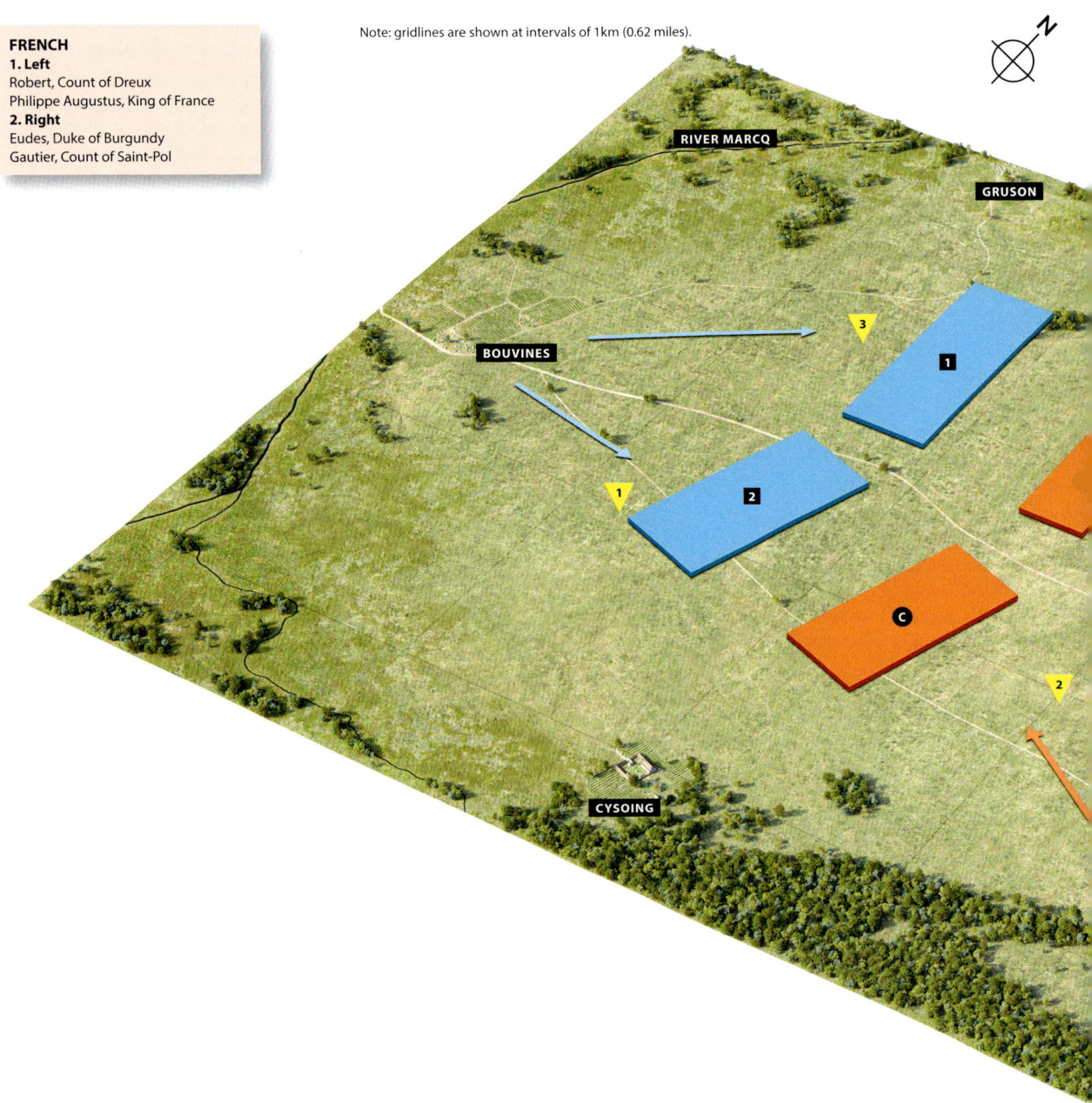

FRENCH
1. Left
Robert, Count of Dreux
Philippe Augustus, King of France
2. Right
Eudes, Duke of Burgundy
Gautier, Count of Saint-Pol

Note: gridlines are shown at intervals of 1km (0.62 miles).

EVENTS

1. Guérin leads a force of horsemen to join the rearguard under Eudes, Duke of Burgundy. This battalion forms a screen, protecting the bridge at Bouvines as the rest of the French army crosses and deploys for battle.

2. The coalition, finding the French ready to engage them, begin to deploy for battle. Their line stretches north, attempting to overlap the French left flank.

3. Philippe Augustus and Robert, Count of Dreux, form a second battalion, extending their line to match the coalition's deployment.

4. Otto IV erects his standard in the coalition's central battalion: a golden eagle over a dragon, mounted on a cart.

5. Renaud, Count of Boulogne, and William, Earl of Salisbury, command the coalition's right battalion.

DEPLOYMENT, BATTLE OF BOUVINES, 27 JULY 1214

The two armies deploy for battle. 'Brother' Guérin's large and well-organized battalion deploys to the south, screening the bridge and the rest of the French army. The coalition, surprised to find the French so well prepared and their own army still strung out along the road from Mortagne, shy away from an immediate attack. Instead they deploy to the east, on open ground suitable for a cavalry engagement, intending to make a single, decisive attack with their whole force. This gives Philippe Augustus time to bring the remainder of his army back across the Marcq and deploy to the north, mirroring the coalition's line of battle.

COALITION
A. Right
Renaud, Count of Boulogne
William, Earl of Salisbury
B. Centre
Otto IV, Emperor of Rome and King of Germany
C. Left
Fernando, Count of Flanders

An illustration of Bouvines from a 15th-century chronicle. Philippe can be identified by his crown and the French royal arms on his shield, coat and caparison. He is jousting with Otto, who is wearing a larger crown and bearing an anachronistic coat of arms. (Photo Josse/Leemage/Corbis via Getty Images)

army whenever it went to war. Richard the Lionheart employed a similar standard at the battle of Arsuf (7 September 1191), where it stood in the very centre of the marching army, protected by a troop of Anglo-Norman noblemen. When the barons of northern England confronted an invading army of Scots at Northallerton on 22 August 1138, Thurstan, Archbishop of York, raised a ship's mast on a wagon and decorated it with holy banners and a pyx (a container for the consecrated host), which acted as both a rallying point and invocation of divine aid. It was considered so important that it gave its name to the encounter: the battle of the Standard.

Apart from Otto himself, only a handful of other individuals in the 'tight-packed formation' around him are identifiable: Bernhard von Horstmar, Gerhart von Randerath, Konrad von Dortmund and Otto von Tecklenburg. They were all close allies who had accompanied him from Germany but they do not seem to have brought many troops with them: Fernando of Flanders had been obliged to escort Otto to the muster at Nivelles in early July with a force of 200 knights, for fear that he would be attacked by the prince-bishop of Liège. It is likely that the majority of this battalion was formed of foot soldiers, either communal militia or professionals, judging by Guillaume le Breton's description of the fighting in this part of the field.

More is known about the French centre, as this is where Philippe Augustus and Guillaume, his chaplain, were stationed. The king's presence was marked by two banners: the royal standard, blue with golden lilies, carried by his household knight, Galon de Montigny, and a simple red banner, the Oriflamme. This banner had first been used by Philippe's grandfather, Louis VI, as he rallied his kingdom to resist the invasion of Emperor Heinrich V, and remained the distinctive military symbol of the French monarchy throughout the Middle Ages. Whenever the king of France went to war, he would first travel to the royal abbey of Saint-Denis to receive the consecrated banner as a symbol of divine aid in the coming campaign. Stationed with the king, 'tasked especially to guard [him]', was a troop of experienced knights. Guillaume le Breton names Barthélemy de Roye (Philippe's grand chamberlain), Gautier the Young (the royal chamberlain), Gérard la Truie, Guillaume de Garlande, Pierre Mauvoisin, Etienne de Longchamp and Philippe's cousin, Henri, Count of Bar, 24 years old and only recently succeeded to the title on the death of his father, Thibaut. The most prominent member of this group was Guillaume des Barres, a man of impeccable military reputation and a career to rival that of his English contemporary, William Marshal. Having learned his craft on the tournament circuit of north-west Europe, he accompanied his master on the Third Crusade, fought in the conquest of Normandy and at the siege of Château Gaillard, and would win enduring fame for his actions at Bouvines. Guillaume le Breton also identifies some of the companies of communal foot soldiers that made up the king's battalion, which deployed in front of the king: Amiens, Arras, Beauvais, Compiègne and Corbie. They were all Picards or Artesians, northerners summoned to defend their king and their homes.

The French right wing appears to have been a purely cavalry force, formed from the troops that had acted as a rearguard that morning and then reinforced when it became clear that the coalition intended to give battle. It was commanded by the man Philippe considered the most able tactician on the field, 'Brother' Guérin. Although he did not fight himself (showing more respect for his ecclesiastical office than Philippe de Dreux), Guillaume le Breton leaves us in no doubt that he directed those who did: '[he] encouraged the warriors and exhorted them to fight for the honour of God, the kingdom and the king, and to defend their own lives'. These knights included Eudes, Duke of Burgundy, who had commanded the army's rearguard, Jean, Count of Beaumont, Guillaume, Count of Sancerre, Adam, Viscount of Melun, and Mathieu de Montmorency.

Another prominent nobleman in this battalion, Gautier de Châtillon, Count of Saint-Pol, reportedly entered the battle under a cloud, as he was

Gautier de Châtillon's arms: *gules, three pallets vair, a chief or* (bottom half: three strips of *vair* on a red field, top half: gold). The blue and white pattern, 'vair', is a heraldic design that represents the squirrel fur used to line cloaks. The skins were sewn together, alternating belly and back fur, creating the unusual 'cup-shaped' pattern. (MostEpic, CC BY-SA 4.0 https://creativecommons.org/licenses/by-sa/4.0, via Wikimedia Commons)

Philippe leads his army in prayer before Bouvines in this 19th-century stained-glass window from St Peter's church, Bouvines. (PIERRE ANDRE LECLERCQ, CC BY-SA 4.0 https://creativecommons.org/licenses/by-sa/4.0/deed.fr, via Wikimedia Commons)

'suspected by some of having supported the enemy at some time' (*Gesta Philippi*). The reasons for this rumour remain obscure. The county of Saint-Pol did share a border with both Boulogne and Flanders, so it would have been unusual if its ruler had not had prior dealings with his two most powerful neighbours. Whatever the cause, the accusation clearly rankled. According to Guillaume le Breton, before the battle Gautier was heard to tell Guérin: 'Today, I will be an honest traitor (*bonus proditor*)'. His subsequent conduct is a testament to the powerful effect that honour and shame could have on the medieval aristocracy. Gautier was no youthful knight errant, eager to establish his reputation: he was solidly middle-aged, a husband and a father, as well as a veteran of crusades in both the Holy Land and Languedoc. Yet he was willing to throw himself into the greatest danger in order to refute the mere rumour that he had behaved improperly.

The coalition's left wing was led by Fernando of Flanders and was made up of knights from Flanders and Hainaut. Using both the chronicle accounts and the *Catalogus Captivorum*, a list of prisoners taken in the battle that was preserved in the French royal registers, we can name many of them. Among the most prominent were Arnoul d'Audenarde (Castellan of Bruges), Hellins de Wavrin (Fernando's seneschal) and Rasse de Gavre (Fernando's butler) and his three sons, Rasse, Arnoul and Philippe, all of whom were captured. Other knights noted by the chroniclers include Gautier de Ghistelle, Buridan de Furnes, Eustace de Machelen and Baudouin de Praet.

Despite the unusually detailed descriptions of the two armies and their dispositions, scholars are unable to agree where three of the most eminent members of the coalition were stationed: Hendrik, Duke of Brabant, Hendrik III, Duke of Limburg, and his son, Waleran, Count of Luxembourg. Verbruggen posits that they never entered the battle at all, reaching the field late in the day and taking flight when they saw the coalition's left and centre start to collapse. A recent study by Sergio Boffa has refuted this, identifying 19 of the prisoners listed in the *Catalogus Captivorum* as either certainly or likely being from Brabant (7 per cent of the total). As the French did not pursue the coalition a great way after the battle, it is reasonable to assume that these men were taken in the fighting itself and therefore Hendrik of Brabant, at least, must have entered the battle with his following, either in the centre near his son-in-law, Otto, or as part of the coalition's right wing.

Guillaume le Breton reports that King Philippe delivered a speech to his army before the battle. Such speeches are a common feature of medieval battle accounts but chroniclers invariably embellish the actual words spoken. The speech given in the *Gesta Philippi* is religious in character and plays heavily on Otto's status as an excommunicate, assuring the French of the righteousness of their cause and that God would inevitably favour them:

> All our hope and faith is set in God; King Otto and his army have been excommunicated by the lord pope, they are enemies and destroyers of the holy Church's property, and the money which provides their wages was acquired from the tears of the poor and the rape of God's Church and His clerics. But we are Christians and delight in communion and peace with the holy Church and, although we are sinners, nevertheless we are in harmony with God's Church and His clerics and defend their liberties with our might. For this reason we should faithfully presume upon God's mercy that, although we are sinners, He will grant that we triumph over our enemies.

Afternoon – the battle

The two armies drawn up in battle array must have been a spectacular sight. Thousands of men and horses, arrayed beneath a rainbow cloud of innumerable banners and pennants: red and blue, yellow and white, lions and fleurs-de-lys. The knights gleamed in the hot summer sun, the light reflecting off steel helms and swords and lanceheads. Guillaume le Breton describes how the two armies stood facing one another, no great distance apart. 'Nobody made a sound', presumably waiting for the trumpet call that would signal the attack.

We do not know exactly what time the battle proper began but it was Guérin, on the French right wing, who made the first offensive manoeuvre. Since 'the Flemings did not deign to advance into the open' (*Philippide*), he despatched a troop of 150 mounted serjeants to attack them. Guillaume le Breton identifies them as men from 'the Soissons valley', vassals or stipendiaries of the abbot of Saint-Médard. The Flemish knights were still deploying and Guérin's plan was to further disrupt them ahead of the main attack: '[this was done] so that these distinguished knights [i.e. the French] would find their enemies a little disturbed and confused' (*Gesta Philippi*). For their part, the Flemish knights took this as an insult and refused to ride forwards to meet the serjeants. Guillaume le Breton attributed this to aristocratic snobbery: they were 'very upset that the first charge against them in the battle was not made by a knight [*miles*], as was proper … since it would be most shameful for those born of noble blood to be defeated by common-born men' (*Philippide*). They had probably expected that there would be some preliminary jousting, in which particularly bold young knights would tilt at one another in the open space between the battle-lines, as regularly occurred during long sieges or before a tournament, but *chevaliers* could not be seen to joust with mere *sergants*. Nevertheless, the serjeants bravely charged the enemy battalion

Knights jousting and falling from the saddle. Young knights fighting single combats between the lines was a celebrated tradition, an opportunity to win fame through one's skill and courage before the confusion of the battle proper. (The Master and Fellows of Trinity College, Cambridge, MS O.9.34 f. 6v)

as they had been ordered. The Flemish knights showed their disdain for the enemy by striking at their unarmoured mounts: '[they] killed most of their horses and wounded many [serjeants], although only two of them were mortally wounded' (*Gesta Philippi*).

The serjeants dealt with, three Flemish knights rode forward, determined to start the battle in the proper style. The sources identify them as Gautier de Ghistelle, Buridan de Furnes and Eustace de Machelen. They shouted encouragement to their comrades, 'urging them to remember their lovers, behaving no differently than if they had been competing in a tournament', while Eustace was shouting, 'Death to the French!' (*Gesta Philippi*). A group of knights from Champagne advanced likewise from the French battalion to engage them. The two sides spurred their horses to the charge, each man gripping his lance under his right arm and aiming to his left, across his horse, with his shield hanging over his left side to protect his body. Jousting in this way required a combination of strength, nerve and superb horsemanship to prevent one's charger swerving away from the enemy at the last moment. Guillaume le Breton describes the particularly gory clash between Eustace de Machelen and a certain Michel de Harmes: Michel thrust his lance clean through Eustace's shield but Eustace aimed lower and Michel 'was pierced through the shield, hauberk and thigh … and he was pinned to his saddle seat and his horse, and both he and his horse fell to the ground' (*Gesta Philippi*). Amazingly, Michel was not killed and managed to secure a fresh horse and continue fighting.

An exceptionally gory battle scene. The knight in the golden helm is wielding an unusual single-edged sword in two hands, possibly a faussard. Roger of Wendover claims that Otto IV used such a weapon at Bouvines. (Morgan MS M.638 f. 10v via ART Collection/Alamy Stock Photo)

It was at this point that the French right wing charged, thousands of horses thundering forward in a great cloud of dust, banners trembling in the breeze. The exact sequence of events is unclear, as Guillaume le Breton presents a series of vignettes – epic deeds performed by certain noblemen and their followers – rather than a clear, sequential narrative but it appears that the knights' charge followed close behind the serjeants' attack, as Guérin had planned. The Anonymous of Béthune, whose account focuses almost solely on events in this part of the battlefield, reports that 'the other side [i.e. the coalition] did not come on as orderly as the French did and this was clear to them'. This agrees with other accounts, in which troops from the French battalion are described as breaking through the Flemish line, wheeling and charging into the enemy rear, which would have been impossible if the battalion had maintained close order.

The gallant Flemish knights who had come out to joust were quickly surrounded and overwhelmed by a troop of Champenois knights, led by one Pierre de Rheims. Gautier and Buridan surrendered and were led away as captives, but Eustace refused to yield, still shouting 'Death to the French!'. Guillaume le Breton describes his fate: 'one [Frenchman] seized him and held his head pressed between his elbow and his breast, another stabbed him in the throat between his chin and hauberk, down into his chest, all the way to the vital parts' (*Gesta Philippi*).

Gautier, Count of Saint-Pol, keen to prove himself a loyal vassal of King Philippe, attacked the enemy with particular ferocity:

> The serjeants who had been sent ahead by the bishop-elect (as we said above) were followed by Gautier, Count of Saint-Pol with the knights chosen by the bishop-elect from among the best. No more gentle than an eagle plunging upon doves, he broke through them, passing through their midst with wonderous speed, striking and hitting many, killing horses and men indifferently, knocking them down and taking no prisoners and so he turned back through another part of the enemy battalion, cutting off as many as possible from the multitude as if in an embrace. (*Gesta Philippi*)

Adam, Viscount of Melun, also performed a textbook attack:

> he assaulted the enemy in the same manner as the count of Saint-Pol in another place and burst through them and returned through the midst of the enemy. There in his battalion Michel de Harmes was pierced through the shield, hauberk and thigh by a certain Fleming, and he was pinned to his saddle seat and his horse and both he and his horse fell to the ground. Hugo de Maleveine fell to the ground and many others, whose horses who had been killed, fell to the ground and then valiantly rose again, fighting no less fiercely on foot than on horseback. he burst through them and returned through the midst of the enemy. (*Gesta Philippi*)

The actions of Eudes, Duke of Burgundy, the most senior nobleman in the French battalion, are very curious. The Anonymous of Béthune reports that he

A king is killed by a sword thrust through the eye slit of his great helm. Contemporary armour was very effective against cutting weapons, so combatants had to target gaps between the mail garments or the opening in the helm to strike a killing blow. (The Master and Fellows of Trinity College, Cambridge, MS O.9.34 f. 34r)

fought 'wearing the coat of arms of Guillaume des Barres, a good knight, but bore his own shield'. It is unclear why he would do this. Swapping one's coat of arms with a lesser knight, or discarding heraldic arms altogether, in order to escape notice was not unknown: Hendrik, Duke of Brabant, had done just this in October 1213 at the battle of the Steppes. But if this was a disguise, why did Eudes retain his shield? The two men carried markedly different arms: Eudes had three diagonal blue stripes on a yellow field, surrounded by a red border (*or three bendlets azure a bordure or*), while des Barres had a diamond pattern in yellow and red (*lozengy or and gules*). Rob Jones has suggested that it may have been intended as a kind of 'Batesian mimicry', like the harmless hoverfly, which has evolved to resemble the dangerous vespid wasp, with Eudes taking on the appearance of the formidable des Barres, perhaps to trick the enemy into thinking that des Barres was in multiple places at once. According to the chronicler, it worked. Arnoul d'Audenarde, Castellan of Bruges, believed that he was facing des Barres:

> And when he saw Eudes approach, he said to his men: 'My lords, see Guillaume des Barres, their good knight, is approaching us. Turn your horses' heads, lest he take us in the flank, for he would do us much harm'. He said this because he thought that the duke was Guillaume des Barres, for he wore his coat of arms. As he said this, the duke came up and Arnoul fought fiercely with him. As they fought with one another, the duke fell and wanted to disembowel [Arnoul's] horse but Arnoul held a dagger in his hand and struck at the eye-slit of the duke's helm, but he fell down and avoided the blow and then fled. (*Chronique des rois*)

This is an example of the brutality that followed the dashing knights' charge: men grappling with one another, daggers in hand, eyes stinging with sweat, desperately stabbing at whatever vulnerable spot they could reach.

Battle scene from the *Life of St Edward* depicting combatants using a variety of hand weapons. Note the two figures in the bottom right, unhorsed but continuing to grapple with one another on the ground, one stabbing the other with a dagger. (Cambridge University Library, MS Ee.3.59, f. 32v via incamerastock/Alamy Stock Photo)

This story might be dismissed as a bit of slander by the anonymous chronicler, whose patron fought in the coalition's left wing at Bouvines and may have enjoyed some bitter laughter at his opponent's expense, but Guillaume le Breton also presents Eudes in a less-than-ideal light. Guillaume does not mention Eudes's coat of arms but he corroborates the *Chronique des rois* in other details, reporting that the duke's horse was killed and that he was knocked to the ground. He had some difficulty regaining his feet, being 'very fat and of a phlegmatic complexion' (a reference to contemporary medical theory: people with an excess of phlegm in their bodies were thought to be lazy and lack enthusiasm). His household knights had to cluster together to protect their fallen lord and lift him bodily onto a fresh mount. Eudes was apparently very angry at losing his horse, and likely embarrassed at being put in such an undignified situation, and proceeded to fight even more fiercely, striking at the enemy 'as if every one of them had killed his horse' (*Gesta Philippi*).

The French right wing had won some great successes but the Flemings fought with great determination. The southern side of the battlefield was now consumed in a general melee. Guillaume le Breton gives us a particularly vivid description that is worth quoting at length from the *Philippide*:

> so many people were mixed up in the fight on the field, finding themselves so close to one another in order to strike and be struck that one could scarcely stretch out a hand in order to make space to strike a stronger blow; and while the silk garments worn over their armour were made with certain distinct insignia, they were open to such blows that now they hung in shreds, utterly destroyed by repeated blows from maces, swords and lances, so that one could scarcely tell friend from foe. This man lies on the ground, legs in the air, another strikes a man in the side, another falls on his head, and his eyes and mouth fill with dirt. Here a knight, there a foot soldier willingly surrenders himself to chains, hating to be killed more than to live in prison. But you can see the horses dying all over the field; some with their bellies cut open, spilling out their guts, others sinking with their legs cut; and others run about without a rider, offering a free mount to anyone who pleases.

The description of horses 'with their bellies cut open' reflects the difficulty of harming a horse protected by a mail caparison. The surest way to kill the horse, and so disadvantage the rider, was to lift its coverings and strike at its unarmoured belly, as Eudes of Burgundy attempted when fighting Arnoul d'Audenarde or as happened to the mount of Renaud, Count of Boulogne, towards the end of the battle.

The Anonymous of Béthune expressed unironic admiration for this scene of carnage, comparing it to a tournament: '[they] had such a good fight that the worthy men who were there testified that they had never seen such good tourneying (*boen tornoiement*) as was done in that part of the battle'. To Guillaume le Breton, expressing a typical cleric's disdain for the sport, it was the Flemings' frivolous conduct at the beginning of the battle, announcing their ladies' names as they came to joust, that was tournament-like. To the anonymous chronicler, however, who may have been a layman and was likely writing for a lay audience, such behaviour was the height of gallantry. They thought the cavalry brawl at Bouvines was a splendid example of its kind, a spectacle of violence usually confined to the artificial world of aristocratic sport.

Tournament from the *Manesse Codex*. The only real indication that this does not depict a true battle is the audience of ladies watching from the stands. From its earliest incarnations, the tournament had a strong erotic element: it was an opportunity for young knights to show off to their sweethearts. (Photo by Fine Art Images/Heritage Images/Getty Image)

    The melee was fierce but not continuous. Gautier, Count of Saint-Pol, was able to retire 'a short way from the fighting' to catch his breath. It was while taking this respite that he noticed that one of his knights had become encircled, with no possibility of escape. Gautier raced forward to rescue him, 'bending low over his horse's neck, grasping its neck with his arm', he broke through the enemy riders. Rising up, he drew his sword and laid about him. The enemies, shocked by this sudden attack, scattered, enabling Gautier to bring his man out of the press 'at extraordinary danger to himself'. Guillaume le Breton claims he heard this story from 'those who were there' (presumably members of Gautier's household) who testified that 'a dozen lances were thrust at [Gautier] at once; but nevertheless they could knock down neither him nor his horse' (*Gesta Philippi*). This was reckless behaviour, especially for a nobleman of Gautier's standing, but also a fine

The earliest visual depiction of Bouvines, by the English monk Matthew Paris. It shows the fallen Philippe (l) being protected by his household knights while Hugues de Boves (r) flees. (Cambridge, Corpus Christi College, MS 16 II f. 41r via World History Archive/Alamy Stock Photo)

display of the reciprocal relationship between lord and vassal, each willing to risk their life to protect the other.

While Fernando was engaged in the southern part of the field, the rest of the coalition army attacked the French. This appears to have been a disjointed charge, given the manoeuvres described, but Otto was able to make significant gains in the centre. According to Guillaume le Breton, the 'warlike and very bold men' of Otto's battalion scattered the communal foot soldiers deployed in front of King Philippe and pushed right through to where the king himself was stationed. The knights appointed to protect him had advanced to engage the enemy, leaving the king behind because they 'feared for his safety'. While they were able to halt the enemy knights, some of the foot soldiers either broke through or bypassed them to attack Philippe himself. They surrounded the king and pulled him from his horse using 'hooks and slender lances'. Guillaume le Breton thought it was a miracle that he was not slain there and then: 'had he not been protected by the right hand of the Most High and his peerless arms, he would have been killed outright' (*Gesta Philippi*). This was the moment of the gravest danger for Philippe, perhaps the most dangerous moment of his long military career. If he had been attacked by knights, he could have expected them to respect chivalrous custom and accept a surrender: at the very least, they would want a share of a literal king's ransom. These foot soldiers, however, were commoners. They could expect no such clemency from their social superiors and would not be eligible to receive a share in any ransom. To them, even the great Augustus was just another enemy to be cut down.

Fortunately for Philippe, some of his household had remained with him. His standard-bearer, Galon de Montigny, signalled for help by 'lowering the standard many times' (*Gesta Philippi*). If an army's standard fell, it was taken as a sign that the battle was lost and everybody should flee, so we can assume that dipping or lowering the standard repeatedly was a sign that the bearer was in extreme danger. While Galon was recalling their comrades, the other knights dismounted to better protect their master, fighting hand-to-hand with the enemy foot soldiers. Guillaume le Breton singles out one Pierre Tristan for his especial valour, '[he] willingly dismounted, exposing himself to many blows, struck down the foot soldiers, scattered and killed them' (*Gesta Philippi*).

We know very little about what was happening in the northern part of the battle at this time. Guillaume le Breton claims that he personally saw

PHILIPPE IS SAVED FROM THE FOOT SOLDIERS, 27 JULY 1214 (PP.74–75)

King Philippe Augustus has been unhorsed and is threatened by enemy foot soldiers, only to be saved by his household knights. This is one of the iconic moments of Bouvines and has been the subject of numerous historical artworks depicting the battle. Philippe is wearing the best armour available: a full hauberk with mail leggings and a great helm that completely encloses his head. This almost certainly saved his life. His surcoat is decorated with the royal arms, golden lily flowers on a blue field (*azure a semi of fleurs-de-lys or*) **(1)**. Medieval knights were far from helpless on foot but the advantages of both speed and height granted by a warhorse meant that they would try to find a fresh mount should theirs be killed. Philippe's household knights have taken the extraordinary step of dismounting in the midst of battle to protect him and help him to his feet **(2)**. On the viewer's left, a servant brings up a fresh horse for the king, protected by a caparison decorated with the royal arms **(3)**.

Pierre Tristan, one of the king's knights, is defending his lord from the enemy foot soldiers **(4)**. They are probably professional soldiers from the Low Countries, given their aggressive behaviour and powerful assault that pierced through to the rear of the French line. They are well armed with a variety of thrusting and cutting weapons, as well as hooks specifically designed to unhorse enemy knights **(5)**. All the coalition army wear white crosses on their chests and backs as a field sign to distinguish them from their enemies.

In the rear of the picture the royal standard-bearer, Galon de Montigny, dips the royal banner as a signal that the king is in danger and the French should rally to his position **(6)**. Command and control was very limited on the medieval battlefield, restricted to trumpets, banners and word of mouth. If a banner fell, it was usually taken as a sign that its owner had been killed or captured, so protecting both the banner and its bearer was crucial.

A cartoon depicting Philippe de Dreux capturing William, Earl of Salisbury, from Beckett's *The Comic History of England* (1894). From the earliest days of the Church, bishops had been forbidden to fight or lead armies but this prohibition was generally ignored. Many bishops had important secular obligations that required them to act as military commanders. (Photo by Print Collector/Getty Images)

the Count of Boulogne's troop attempt to attack King Philippe's position but 'he turned back, withdrew from him and engaged Robert, Count of Dreux' (*Gesta Philippi*). Perhaps Renaud was meant to attack in concert with Otto's battalion but the emperor advanced too quickly and blocked him from engaging the French centre. This would agree with the reports that the coalition's attack was generally uncoordinated. Or, it may be that Robert de Dreux interposed his battalion between Renaud and the French centre to protect the king. There was certainly some hand-to-hand fighting taking place:

> [Philippe], Bishop of Beauvais, was grieved to see the king of England's own brother (who, since he was a man of remarkable strength, the English gave him the name 'Longsword') scatter the men of Dreux and inflict bloody injures on his brother's battalion; and since he held a club [*clava*] in his strong hand, concealing that he was a bishop, struck him on the top of his head, breaking his helmet, compelled him to fall to the ground, to mark the earth with the imprint of his long body. (*Philippide*)

There then followed an almost farcical scene in which Philippe (perhaps recalling that it

A knight and a king wrestle on horseback. It is unclear who is trying to capture whom. The knight may be trying to hold on to the king, or the king may be trying to pull his opponent out of the saddle (note his right hand holding the knight's belt). (The Master and Fellows of Trinity College, Cambridge, MS O.9.34 f. 18r)

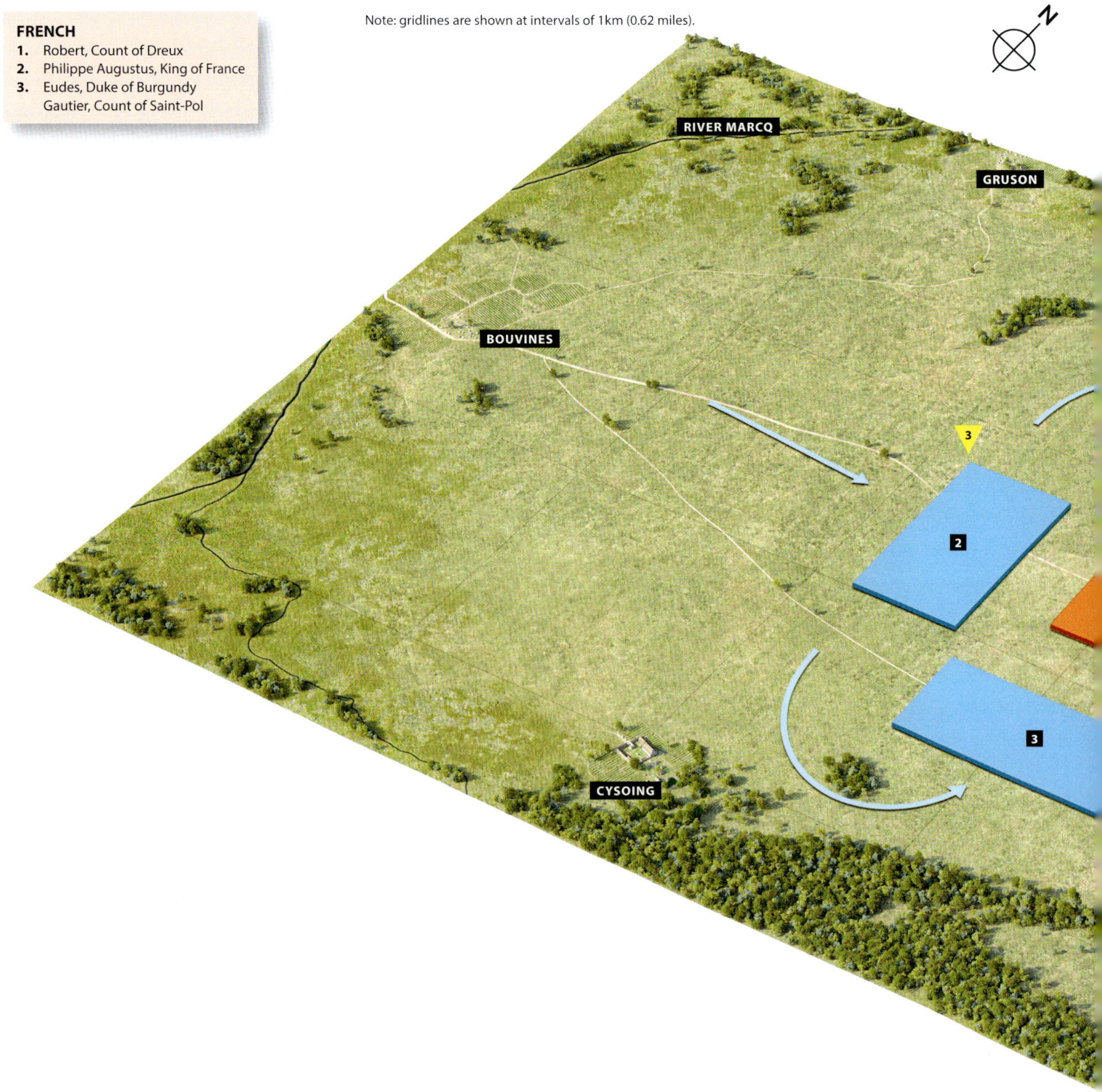
FRENCH
1. Robert, Count of Dreux
2. Philippe Augustus, King of France
3. Eudes, Duke of Burgundy
Gautier, Count of Saint-Pol
Note: gridlines are shown at intervals of 1km (0.62 miles).
N
RIVER MARCQ
GRUSON
BOUVINES
3
2
3
CYSOING

EVENTS

1. The coalition army, panicked by the sight of the emperor falling back from an attack by the French centre, flees. Otto escapes on a fresh mount but many knights in the left battalion, including Fernando of Flanders, are taken prisoner.

2. Renaud, Count of Boulogne, performs a rearguard action to protect his retreating allies. His Brabançon foot soldiers form a ring, holding off the enemy knights with their long spears, while Renaud leads his troop of knights on forays, retreating behind the foot to rest.

3. The French army surround the coalition's rearguard. Renaud is captured when his horse is killed under him. Philippe Augustus orders Thomas de Saint-Valéry to assault the Brabançons. They are overwhelmed by a combined attack of knights and foot soldiers.

DEFEAT, BATTLE OF BOUVINES, 27 JULY 1214

Towards the end of the battle, the coalition's left wing has been overwhelmed and Fernando, Count of Flanders, captured along with many of his knights. Likewise William, Earl of Salisbury, has been captured by the Bishop of Beauvais on the right. Otto IV has escaped an attack by the French in the centre but the sight of him retreating to find a fresh mount creates panic, causing the coalition army to retreat east. Renaud, Count of Boulogne, commands the rearguard: a formidable formation of Brabançon foot soldiers armed with long spears. The French surround Renaud and eventually overwhelm his men through force of numbers.

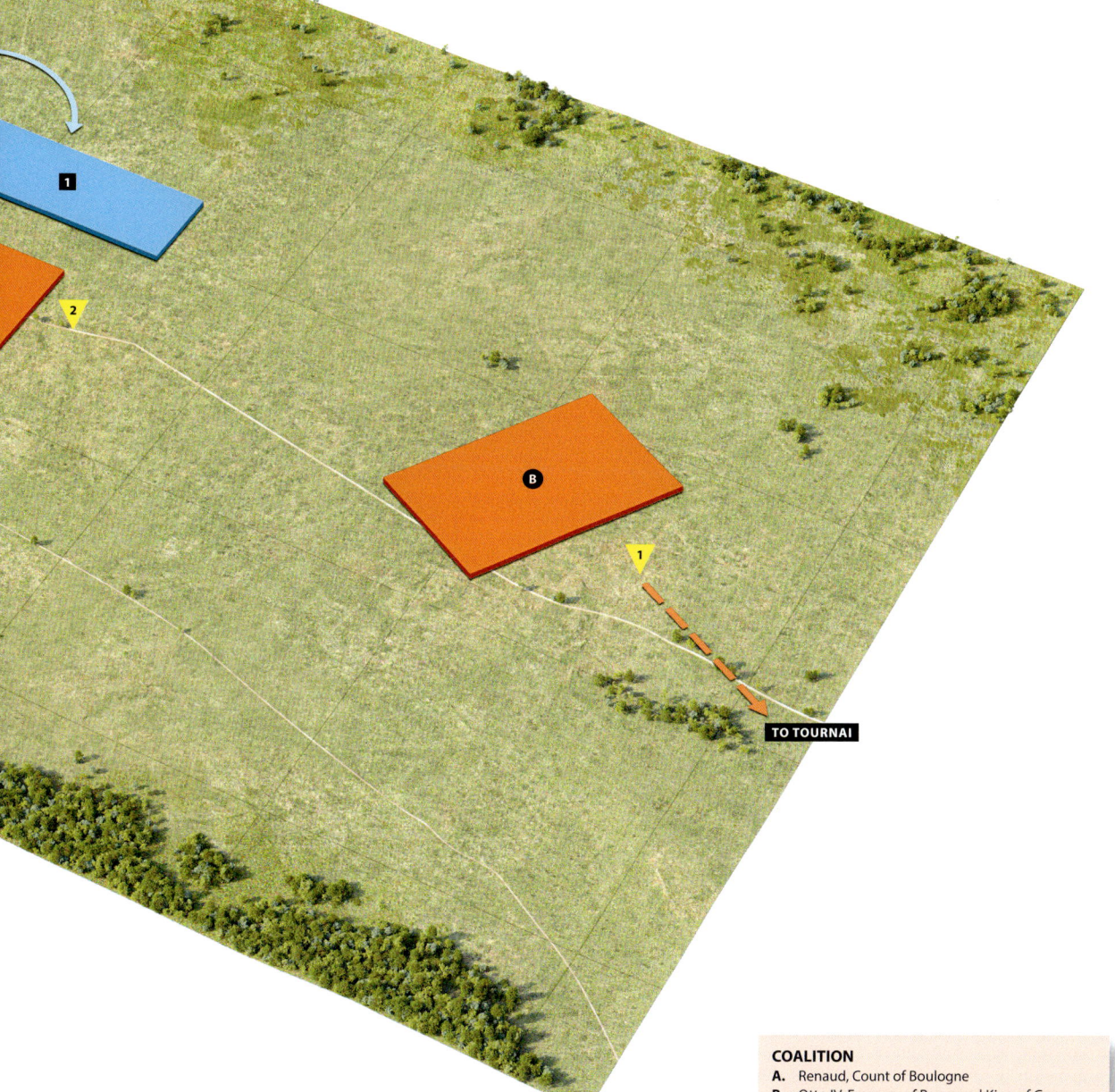

COALITION
A. Renaud, Count of Boulogne
B. Otto IV, Emperor of Rome and King of Germany

A victorious army drives its enemies before it. In theory, custom protected knightly combatants from being killed outright but nothing could be guaranteed in the chaos of battle. Moreover, a prisoner's ransom could ruin a family for generations. To preserve life and fortune, many fled. (Morgan MS M.638 f. 10r via Jimlop collection/Alamy Stock Photo)

was not quite appropriate for a bishop to be fighting in this way) asked another man, Jean de Nivelle, to bind the fallen earl and pretend that de Nivelle had captured him.

In the centre, King Philippe's household knights were able to raise him to his feet and secure a fresh mount for him. With the king safe and the foot soldiers who had threatened him dead or withdrawn, Guillaume des Barres led the knights in a fierce counter-attack on the coalition's centre. Cutting their way through the press, they reached Otto's own troop. Now it was Otto who was in serious danger, assailed by multiple skilful and determined professional soldiers. Pierre Mauvoisin, whom Guillaume le Breton says was noted more for his skill in arms than his prudence, managed to seize the bridle of Otto's horse but was 'unable to pull him out of the formation that surrounded him'. Gérard la Truie actually struck the emperor in the chest with his dagger but did not penetrate his hauberk. He drew back his arm for a second blow, only for Otto's horse to throw up its head: 'the dagger passed through the horse's eye and struck its brain' (*Gesta Philippi*). The poor animal, terrified and in great pain, turned and fled, taking Otto with it. His men brought up a fresh horse for him but the French knights gave them no respite, pursuing vigorously. Guillaume des Barres led the chase, actually grasping Otto by the neck twice, but 'the speed of his horse and the density of his knights' [formation]' saved him. Guillaume des Barres's horse was killed under him but he quickly got to his feet. He defied the enemies who surrounded him, fighting bravely on foot until he was rescued by a company led by Thomas de Saint-Valéry, one of the many de Dreux relatives fighting for the French that day.

This appears to have been the turning point of the battle. We do not know which part of the coalition army was the first to flee. The anonymous chronicler from the abbey of Saint-Bertin says that it was the communal foot soldiers from Bruges. The Anonymous of Béthune claims that it was Hendrik of Brabant. Guillaume le Breton says that Otto himself was 'among the first to flee', followed closely by Hendrik of Brabant, Waleran of Luxembourg and Hugues de Boves, the bellicose captain who had urged the coalition to give battle and accused Renaud de Dammartin of cowardice. Hendrik's commitment to the coalition was tenuous at best and it is plausible that he withdrew as soon as the battle seemed to be favouring the French. We know that Fernando was captured in the fighting in the southern part of the field, along with many of his knights, but it is unclear whether this happened before or after other elements of the army, which were less heavily engaged than the left wing, had already begun to retreat. Given Guillaume le Breton's account of the attack on Otto's battalion, and his withdrawal to find a fresh horse, it was probably the sight of the emperor and his men falling back in the face of a determined French attack that convinced many that the battle was lost and they should look to their own safety.

There was no rout, however. Guillaume le Breton's account suggests that a rearguard was formed to protect Otto and the other troops as they withdrew east. He describes how the battle 'revived once more' and names four German knights who were still fighting as the emperor fled: Konrad von Dortmund, Bernhard von Horstmar, Gerhart von Randerath and Otto von Tecklenburg. The emperor escaped but his allies were eventually overwhelmed by superior French numbers. Bernhard and Gerhart were captured and the French tore down the imperial eagle standard: a sure sign that Otto had been defeated.

The most famous, and formidable, part in this rearguard action was played by Renaud de Dammartin, Count of Boulogne. Although he had only six knights left in his troop, he still commanded a company of Brabançon foot soldiers, which he deployed to great effect:

> The count of Boulogne employed a remarkable piece of skill: he made for himself something like a wall of armed serjeants and crowded them together into two lines like a wheel that resembled a castle under siege, where there was an entrance like a gate where he was received whenever he wished to recover his breath or he was hard pressed by his enemies, and he did this many times.
> (*Gesta Philippi*)

Baldwin describes this as an 'unusual tactic' but other contemporary accounts describe foot soldiers using similar formations. The *Histore de Gille de Chyn*, a lesser-known romance composed in Hainaut in the first part of the 13th century, described a (fictitious) war between Brabant and Hainaut: 'Nevertheless the men of Brabant resolutely and determinedly placed themselves in a ring, but none of our men could move them, for they lowered their heads in determination. Each man raised his weapon to hold back and resist those who wished to attack them.' This required a high degree of discipline and resolve from the foot soldiers, especially when they found themselves isolated and facing the main strength of the French army alone. They were armed with long spears and the French knights were unable to reach them: 'since they themselves fought with swords and short weapons' (*Philippide*). The difficulty that this formation caused the French is further evidence that both sides lacked a significant number of missile weapons: the French could not eliminate the Brabançons except by a close assault, nor

RENAUD DE DAMMARTIN SALLIES OUT FROM BEHIND HIS BRABANÇONS, 27 JULY 1214 (PP.82–83)

Renaud, Count of Boulogne, forms the rearguard of the coalition army with a company of Brabançons. These tough, professional foot soldiers have formed a ring, 'like a castle', protected from the enemy knights by their long spears **(1)**. They are well protected with mail coats or padded cloth jackets (*gambesons*) and steel helmets, making an almost-impenetrable obstacle to the French, who lack the missile weapons to harass them from afar. There is a narrow gap in the ring, which Renaud has been using to ride in and out of the formation **(2)**. He leads his remaining knights on forays to attack the French, retreating behind his foot soldiers to rest or to escape when heavily pressed. Guillaume le Breton noted the unusual crest he wore on his helm: two 'horns' made of baleen, 'waving in the breeze, taken from the black ribs which the whale dwelling in the sea of Brittany bears in its cavernous gills' **(3)**. Such crests were unusual in the early 13th century but would become more common in the following centuries, particularly in the theatrical world of the tournament. Renaud is followed by one of his household knights, bearing a banner decorated with the Dammartin arms: silver and blue stripes surrounded by a red border (*barry of argent and azure, a bordure gules*) **(4)**. According to Guillaume le Breton, Renaud had sworn to Hugues de Boves, who had accused him of treachery, that he would 'either die fighting or be captured' that day.

Bouvines, as depicted in a 14th-century French royal chronicle. As in other illuminations depicting the battle, it is portrayed as a purely cavalry affair with Philippe and Otto as the foremost participants. The foot soldiers who made up the majority of both armies are absent. (The History Collection/Alamy Stock Photo)

could they move off or effectively attack their enemies without breaking their tight formation. It was left to Renaud de Dammartin and his handful of cavalry to take the offensive, sallying out of the ring to attack the French and then return to safety.

It was during one of these forays that Renaud was finally captured. A knight named Pierre de la Tournelle, fighting on foot because his horse had been killed, succeeded in getting close enough to Renaud to 'lift up his horse's covering and thrust his sword up to the hilt into the horse's stomach' (*Gesta Philippi*). Renaud, apparently heedless to the danger, tried to fight on. Ignoring his lord's protests, one of Renaud's household knights seized the horse's reins and drew it away from the fighting, only to be knocked down himself by the brothers Quenon and Jean de Coudun. Renaud's horse finally collapsed. Unable to leap clear in time, he was left prostrate, his leg pinned under the horse's neck. There now began a quarrel between the French about who should actually claim Renaud as their prisoner. This was a serious matter, as the man who brought Renaud to King Philippe could expect both great honour and material reward. At least one of those present, however, thought that Renaud did not deserve the dignity of surrender. Guillaume le Breton says that a 'young ruffian' (*garcio*) named 'Cornutus' tore off Renaud's helm and 'gave him a great wound in the face' with his sword, before attempting a killing stroke by trying to stab his 'lower parts' with a dagger. Renaud survived only because his mail leggings 'were sewn into the lining of his hauberk' and Cornutus was unable to find a gap before he was restrained by his companions.

While the knights were arguing among themselves, Renaud spotted 'Brother' Guérin nearby, whom he knew from his time at the royal court. He cried out that he would surrender to Guérin, provided that his life was spared. With characteristic duplicity, he immediately reneged on this promise when he saw an ally, Arnoul d'Audenarde (who had unhorsed the Duke of Burgundy earlier in the battle), riding up with a troop of knights: 'he feigned that he was unable to stand up, and deliberately tumbled to the ground, expecting them to help him' (*Gesta Philippi*). But the French were not to

A corpse, wrapped in a shroud, is removed from the battlefield. Very few noblemen were recorded as killed at Bouvines. A later chronicler claims that the dead were buried at the nearby monastery of Cysoing, while the wounded were taken to Douai. (The Master and Fellows of Trinity College, Cambridge, O.9.34 f. 11v)

be denied their prize. With 'redoubled blows', they forced Renaud to mount a packhorse to be led away, while Arnoul and his men, far from rescuing Renaud, were themselves taken prisoner.

Despite the loss of their commander, the Brabançon foot, 'who had placed themselves like a wall', continued to hold out, even as the French began to pillage the coalition's baggage. They were finally overwhelmed when Philippe ordered Thomas de Saint-Valéry to attack them with 50 horsemen and 2,000 foot soldiers: 'he assaulted them with great fury and massacred them entirely' (*Gesta Philippi*).

The battle of Bouvines lasted for about three hours. King Philippe did not permit his men to pursue those fleeing 'on account of the unknown terrain and the approaching nightfall' (*Gesta Philippi*), suggesting that the fighting did not begin until mid-afternoon. He was also very concerned that the high-status prisoners he had taken should not escape or be rescued in the confusion. The most important captives were Renaud, Count of Boulogne, William, Earl of Salisbury, and Fernando, Count of Flanders, who had been 'pierced with many wounds, knocked to the ground and led away captive, and most of his knights with him' (*Gesta Philippi*).

The total number of casualties on either side is difficult to judge, given the partial nature of the records, but among the aristocracy, they seem to have been low, in keeping with other High Medieval battles. Guillaume le Breton reports that the French captured five counts and 25 knights-banneret, with the total number of prisoners taken estimated at 300 or more. Very few senior noblemen were reportedly killed outright. One exception is Etienne de Longchamp, one of Philippe's household knights, who was killed 'before the king's own eyes' when a dagger was thrust into the eye slit of his helm. Of the mounted serjeants and foot soldiers we know nothing, but their losses were probably significant. They were less heavily armed than the knights and would not be ransomed if taken alive, which meant they were likely to be killed out of hand.

AFTERMATH

King Philippe had won a clear victory but at least one person believed that the coalition's cause might still be salvaged. It was rumoured that Renaud de Dammartin, despite being imprisoned, had been able to send a message to Otto shortly after the battle, advising him to retreat to Ghent, reform the army and continue the campaign from there. Philippe was so angry when he heard this that he went to visit Renaud in person and berated him, listing his many betrayals and acts of ingratitude, even after Philippe had spared his life: 'You did all this to me; nevertheless, I will not take your life from you; but you will not leave prison until you have made amends for all these things' (*Gesta Philippi*). Renaud was taken to Péronne and confined in chains. Despite the petitions submitted by his wife, Ida, he was never released. He took his own life in prison in April 1227.

Otto did not renew the campaign in 1214. He had failed to achieve anything by joining his uncle's coalition and returned to Brunswick, defeated and humiliated. Philippe Augustus sent the golden eagle that had adorned Otto's standard as a gift to his rival, Friedrich II. Shortly after Bouvines, the key German cities of Cologne and Aachen fell to Friedrich, finally ending any hope that Otto may have had of reclaiming his empire. He died in 1218, living out his last years on his family estates in Brunswick, the first and only Welf emperor of Germany.

Renaud's fellow prisoner, Fernando of Flanders, was paraded through Paris in chains, before being confined in the Louvre. He was to remain a French prisoner for the next 12 years, only released on the death of Louis VIII and the accession of Blanche of Castile as queen-regent. William, Earl of Salisbury, the other senior prisoner taken at Bouvines, was quickly ransomed in exchange for Robert III de Dreux, son of Robert II and nephew to the bishop who had knocked William on the head in the battle. He would go on to play a prominent role in the civil war between his brother John and the English barons and in the early years of Henry III's reign.

Following his triumphal return to Paris, Philippe reunited with Louis and headed south to confront John. The Angevin king was reportedly very angry when he learned of the defeat at Bouvines but did not abandon his position at La Rochelle, preferring to wait for reinforcements from England. At Loudun, Philippe received the submission of Aimery, Viscount of Thouars, and through him the leading barons of Poitou and Aquitaine. It was only now that John admitted that the campaign was over and sent messengers to Philippe to open negotiations. A truce was agreed at Chinon on 18 September. It was to last for five years from the following Easter and in return John was

An imaginative, if anachronistic, depiction of Fernando being paraded through Paris (the armour worn by Philippe's retinue is far too late for 1214). Executing noble prisoners was taboo in this period but Philippe was still able to publicly humiliate Fernando. Engraving from the *Histoire populaire de la France* (1880). (Photo by Leemage/Corbis via Getty Images)

to pay Philippe 60,000 marks. John sailed from La Rochelle at the beginning of October, never to return to the Continent.

For military historians, Bouvines is a prototypical example of that rare occurrence: a set-piece battle of the High Middle Ages. Few battles of this period are as vividly recorded as Bouvines: few provide us with such a wealth of information about strategy, equipment, tactics or military ethos. It demonstrates the limitations – in logistics, intelligence, command and control – that gave medieval warfare its unique character, as well as the surprising sophistication that could still be achieved at different levels.

Guillaume le Breton makes it clear that the true mastermind of the French victory was not Philippe but his advisor, 'Brother' Guérin. It was his reconnaissance on the morning of 27 July that alerted the French to the coalition's presence, he who urged the king to give battle and he who organized the crucial cavalry action on the French right that protected the rest of the army as it crossed the Marcq. In all this, he was aided by the cohesion within the French army: all the senior commanders were obedient to their king's orders and fought loyally for him. The coalition's attack, by contrast, was ambitious in concept but disjointed in execution. Not only did they lack a clear commander-in-chief, the various individuals who made up the army's senior command did not trust one another and displayed varying levels of commitment to the cause. In a political and military culture that relied heavily on personal leadership, this was their fundamental weakness. A smaller, more cohesive army might have succeeded in catching the rear of the French army unprepared as it marched to Lille but both the pursuit and the eventual attack were poorly coordinated.

At the tactical level, Bouvines provides clear evidence of the importance of coherency within a medieval army and the effect that a well-led tactical unit could have, whether that be Gautier de Châtillon's cavalry making

Bouvines remains a 'key date' in French history, a milestone in the development of the French monarchy and, by extension, the nation of France. Images of Philippe Augustus at Bouvines have been produced in books, paintings, even chocolate adverts like this one from the 19th century. (Photo by Art Media/Print Collector/Getty Images)

repeated charges into the Flemings or Renaud de Dammartin's defiant infantry formation. The accounts also remind us that, for all the romance and glamour attached to this period, the reality of hand-to-hand fighting with medieval equipment was as vicious as any time in human history.

THE CONSEQUENCES OF BOUVINES AND MAGNA CARTA

Bouvines stands as one of the most important battles in European history. Philippe Augustus's victory established him as the premier ruler of Western Europe and shaped the future of France for centuries to come. French kings would no longer be confined to a small parcel of territory around Paris, their authority ignored or outright opposed by their own magnates. The Capetians were masters of northern France and, within a generation, they had assumed direct rule over much of the Languedoc as well. Henceforth they would provide strong, centralized government for their kingdom, concentrating lands and titles that had previously belonged to other families within their own dynasty. This form of French monarchy would shape the course of European history for centuries to come, just as its violent overthrow in the 18th century continues to shape our world today.

The consequences of Bouvines were equally profound for John and England. The campaign had been an utter failure. John had bled his subjects dry to pay for his war. In itself, this was nothing new to the English barons: Henry II and Richard had both been grasping, exploitative rulers. However,

An engraving from Doyle's *A Chronicle of England* (1864) depicts John 'signing' Magna Carta. This reflects a common misconception: in keeping with standard royal practice, John did not *sign* Magna Carta but authenticated it with his seal. (incamerastock/Alamy Stock Photo)

they had never behaved so arbitrarily, never demanded so much and yet achieved so little. Had John returned from the Continent in triumph, had he compelled Philippe to restore his ancestral lands and to pay him recompense for the loss, he might have been able to pay off or overawe his barons. As it was, he returned weaker and poorer than ever to face a war with his own tenants-in-chief.

Attempts to negotiate in early 1215 failed. John summoned his barons to a council at Oxford in April but they did not attend, choosing instead to muster their army at Stamford, Lincolnshire. On 5 May, the rebels defied John, openly renouncing their homage to him. Less than two weeks later, London opened its gates to the rebel army, which now contained some of the most powerful men in England. Yet for all their successes, the rebels had achieved no more than a stalemate: John held too many royal castles for them to win a quick, decisive victory, and John could not hope to take London by siege. So, another round of negotiations began. On 15 June at Runnymede, a neutral site on the Thames halfway between London and John's castle at Windsor, John and the rebel barons met to seal an agreement to end their conflict, an agreement that came to be called Magna Carta.

It is important to remember that Magna Carta was a product of a particular situation and set of circumstances. It was not intended as a blueprint for fundamentally restructuring the kingdom, still less a statement of universal

One of four surviving copies of the 1215 Magna Carta, on display at Salisbury Cathedral. Multiple copies of the text were made at Runnymede and sent to bishops across England who were to disseminate the content of the charter to their dioceses. (Photo by Finnbarr Webster/Getty Images)

rights and principles. It was a compromise, negotiated between a king and his aristocratic tenants-in-chief. Nevertheless, as David Carpenter has observed, the agreement imposed 'unprecedented and profound' restrictions on English kingship. The barons sought to impose limits on John's ability to raise revenue, to fine or punish his subjects arbitrarily and to influence elections to Church offices. If he would not abide by these conditions, a committee of 25 barons was to be appointed with the power to compel him, by force if necessary.

As one might expect, John had no intention of abiding by the agreement. He immediately appealed to Pope Innocent, his overlord since doing homage to the papal legate in 1213. The pope obliged by issuing a bull in August 1215 that condemned Magna Carta and threatened to excommunicate those who tried to enforce it. The rebels, realizing that John would never negotiate in good faith, declared him deposed and invited Louis, son of Philippe

Augustus, to take the throne. The peace that Magna Carta was meant to guarantee lasted less than 12 weeks. When John died at Newark-on-Trent in October 1216, he left England in the midst of a bloody civil war between his supporters and the rebels under Louis.

John may have agreed to Magna Carta in bad faith but his death secured its place in English law. John's son and heir, Henry III, was only nine years old at the time of his father's death and unable to govern. Royal authority was instead invested in a council of regents, led by William Marshal, Earl of Pembroke. No longer bound by John's intransigence, and militarily secure after victory in the battles of Lincoln (20 May 1217) and Sandwich (24 August 1217), the regents reissued Magna Carta in the boy king's name, and with the agreement of the papal legate, in November 1217 as part of a reconciliation between the rebels and the Crown. It was a less radical document than the one sealed at Runnymede (crucially, the 'security clause' empowering a committee of 25 barons to oversee the king had been removed) but it was still a moment of great significance. It was a pledge, on behalf of the boy king, to govern with justice, under the law, on behalf of the whole community of the realm. Henry made sure to reissue Magna Carta again in his own right when he came of age in 1225, when it finally achieved the status of law.

The legacy of Magna Carta is frequently overstated. The actual details of the agreement were politically irrelevant within a few generations. Only four of the original 63 clauses remain a part of English law today. Nor was it a uniquely 'English' creation, produced by that culture's exceptional regard for liberty and freedom; it was heavily influenced by ideas from both contemporary Europe and ancient Roman law. None of this is to deny its power as a symbol, however. It codified concepts that would have a profound impact on the English-speaking world for centuries to come: of the realm as a commonwealth where everybody is subject to the same laws, of the need for consensus between the government and the governed, of sovereign authority operating under appropriate restraints. The principles contained (or believed to be contained) in Magna Carta shaped the conflict between England's king and parliament in the 17th century, the American colonies' struggle for independence in the 18th and even the devolpment of the principle of universal human rights in the 20th. It is far too simplistic to draw a straight line between these grand milestones in human history and a single battle but, had John persuaded his allies to fight at Roche-aux-Moines, had the coalition caught the French on the march to Lille, had Philippe died when the common foot soldiers dragged him from his horse, the events of 1215 and beyond could have been very different. In that sense, Bouvines is the battle that gave the world Magna Carta and everything that followed.

BIBLIOGRAPHY AND FURTHER READING

PRIMARY SOURCES

Anonymous of Béthune, 'Chronique française des rois de France', in *Recueil des historiens des Gaules et de la France*, Vol. XXIV, Paris (1904), pp.750–76

'Ex Historiis Anonymi Remensis', ed. by O. Holder Egger, in *Monumenta Germaniae Historica*, Scriptores, SS 26, Hanover (1882), pp.523–55

'Flandria Generosa usque ad a. 1164', ed. by D. L. C. Bethmann, in *Monumenta Germaniae Historica*, Scriptores, SS 9, Hanover (1851), pp.313–34

Guillaume le Breton, *La Philippide*, trans. by François Guizot, Paris (1825)

Oeuvres de Rigord et de Guillaume le Breton: Historiens de Philippe-Auguste, ed. by François Delaborde, 2 vols, Paris (1882–85)

Ralph of Coggeshall, *Chronicon Anglicanum*, ed. by Joseph Stevenson, London (1875)

Roger of Wendover, *Chronica sive Flores Historiarum*, ed. by Henry Coxe, 4 vols, London (1841–44)

SECONDARY MATERIAL

Aurell, Martin, 'La Bataille de la Roche-aux-Moines: Jean sans terre et la prétendue traîtrise des Poitevins', in *Comptes rendus des séances de l'Académie des Inscriptions et Belles-Lettres*, CLXI.I (2017), pp.465–89

Baldwin, John W., *The Government of Philip Augustus: Foundations of French Royal Power in the Middle Ages*, Berkeley, CA: University of California Press (1986)

Baldwin, John W., *Knights, Lords and Ladies: In Search of Aristocrats in the Paris Region 1180–1220*, Philadelphia, PA: University of Pennsylvania Press (2019)

Barthélemy, Dominique, *La Bataille de Bouvines: Histoire et légendes*, Paris (2018)

Boffa, Sergio, 'Le Rôle équivoque joué par le duc de Brabant Henri Ier à la bataille de Bouvines (27 juillet 1214)', in *Cahiers de civilisation médiévale*, LIX (2016), pp.337–56

Boffa, Sergio, 'Les Mercenaires appelés "Brabançons" aux ordres de Renaud de Dammartin et leur tactique défensive à la bataille de Bouvines (1214)', in *Revue du Nord*, DCXIX (2017), pp.7–24

Bradbury, Jim, *Philip Augustus: King of France 1180–1223*, London: Routledge (1998)

Contamine, Philippe, 'L'armée de Philippe Auguste', in *La France de Philippe Auguste: Le Temps des mutations*, Paris: CNRS (1982), pp.578–94

Duby, Georges, *The Legend of Bouvines: War, Religion and Culture in the Middle Ages*, trans. by Catherine Tihanyi, Berkeley, CA: University of California Press (1990)

France, John, *Western Warfare in the Ages of the Crusades 1000–1300*, London: UCL Press (1999)

France, John, *Medieval France at War: A Military History of the French Monarchy 885–1305*, York: Arc Humanities Press (2022)

France, John (ed.), *Mercenaries and Paid Men: The Mercenary Identity in the Middle Ages*, Leiden: Brill (2008)

Goldman, Lawrence (ed.), *Magna Carta: History, Context and Influence*, London: UOL Press (2018)

Holt, J. C., *Magna Carta*, 3rd edn, Cambridge: Cambridge University Press (2015)

Jordan, Erin L., 'The "Abduction" of Ida of Boulogne: Assessing Women's Agency in Thirteenth-Century France', in *French Historical Studies*, Vol. XXX.I (2007) pp.1–20

McGlynn, Sean, *Blood Cries Afar: The Magna Carta War and the Invasion of England 1215–1217*, Stroud: Spellmount (2011)

Malo, Henri, *Un grand feudataire: Renaud de Dammartin et la coalition de Bouvines*, Paris (1898)

Turner, Ralph, *King John*, London: Longman, London (1994)

Verbruggen, J. F., *The Art of Warfare in Western Europe during the Middle Ages*, trans. by Sumner Willard and R. W. Southern, 2nd edn, Woodbridge: Boydell (1997)

FURTHER READING

The primary sources for Bouvines remain somewhat difficult for English-speaking readers to access. Georges Duby's *The Legend of Bouvines* contains the only published English translation of the *Gesta Philippi*'s account of Bouvines. Readers should be advised that this is not a very precise translation, as it is Catherine Tihanyi's 1990 translation of Duby's 1973 French rendering of Guillaume le Breton's Latin. *The Legend* also contains English versions of other primary source material, either via Duby in the case of Latin texts, or directly from the Old French. These can be accessed for free on the website for *The Society for Medieval Military History*. There is as yet no complete published version of the *Philippide* in English but Guizot's French translation is currently available online for free and helps to make this particularly dense Latin poem more accessible.

For the wider context of the Angevin–Capetian conflict and Magna Carta, see:

Carpenter, David, *The Struggle for Mastery: Britain 1066–1284*, London: Penguin (2004)

Church, Stephen, *King John: England, Magna Carta, and the Making of a Tyrant*, London: Macmillan (2015)

Gillingham, John, *The Angevin Empire*, 2nd edn, London: Bloomsbury (2001)

Hanley, Catherine, *Two Houses, Two Kingdoms: A History of France and England 1100–1300*, London: Yale University Press (2022)

Huscroft, Richard, *Tales from the Long Twelfth Century: The Rise and Fall of the Angevin Empire*, New Haven, CT: Yale University Press (2016)

For warfare in the High Middle Ages, see:

Crouch, David, *William Marshal*, 3rd edn, London: Routledge (2016)

Davis, R. H. C, *The Medieval Warhorse: Origin, Development and Redevelopment*, London: Thames & Hudson (1989)

DeVries, Kelly and Kay Douglas Smith, *Medieval Military Technology*, 2nd edn, North York, ON: Broadview Press (2012)

Gravett, Christopher, *Medieval Siege Warfare*, Oxford: Osprey (1990)

Jones, Rob, *Bloodied Banners: Martial Display on the Medieval Battlefield*, Woodbridge: Boydell (2010)

Keen, Maurice (ed.), *Medieval Warfare: A History*, Oxford: Oxford University Press (1999)

Nicolle, David, *French Medieval Armies 1000–1300*, Oxford: Osprey (1991)

Nicolle, David, *European Medieval Tactics (1): The Fall and Rise of Cavalry 450–1260*, Oxford: Osprey (2011)

Smail, R. C., *Crusading Warfare 1097–1193*, 2nd edn, Cambridge: Cambridge University Press (1994)

Strickland, Matthew, *War and Chivalry: The Conduct and Perception of War in England and Normandy, 1066–1217*, Cambridge: Cambridge University Press (1996)

Titterton, James, *Deception in Medieval Warfare: Trickery and Cunning in the Central Middle Ages*, Woodbridge: Boydell (2022)

INDEX

Figures in **bold** refer to illustrations.

Acre, siege of 17, **17**
Adam, Viscount of Melun 36, 55–56, 57, 65, 69
Aire 13–14, 18
ambushes 56–57, **56**
Angers 43, 45
Angevin Empire 5–7, 12, 14, 28
Anjou 5, 6, 11, 22, 45
Aquitaine 5, 10, 12, 17
armour 31–34, 36, **46–48**, **69**, **74–76**, 82–84
Arnoul d'Audenarde 66, 70, 71, 85–86
Arthur of Brittany 11–12
Artois 14, 18, 24, 36
Assize of Arms (1181) 36

banners **59**, 60, 61, 65, 76, 82–84
Baudouin IX of Flanders 13
Bernhard von Horstmar 64, 81
Blanche of Castile **25**, 87
Boulogne 14, 25, 44
Bouvines battle 52–86, **56**, **64**, **73**, **85**, **89**
 morning 54–58
 afternoon, deployment 58–67
 afternoon, the battle 67–86
 aftermath 87–89
 casualties 86, **86**
 consequences of 89–92
 sources 52, 54
 tactical lessons 88–89
Brabançon (or Brabanter) 29–31, 36, 78–79, 81–85, 86
Buridan de Furnes 66, 68, 69

Capetians 5, 13, 28, 52, 58, 89
Catalogus Captivorum 40, 66
Château Gaillard 6, **6**, 14, 18
Chronique des rois de France 37, 54, 57, 60, 69–70, 71, 81
Clément, Henri 25, 44–45
coats of arms **21**, 33, 39, **39**, 61, **61**, **64**, 70
Codex Manesse 45, **72**
commanders
 coalition 10–16
 French 16–21
Cornutus 85
crossbowmen 37, **46–48**, 57
crusades 17, 18, 19, 20, 34, 35

Damme 6, 18

Eleanor of Aquitaine 5, 11
Enguerrand Brisemoutier 45–49, **46–48**
Etienne de Longchamp 65, 86
Eudes III, Duke of Burgundy 57, 62–63, 65, 69–71, 78–79
Eustace de Machelen 66, 68, 69

Fernando, Count of Flanders and Hainaut **13**, 13–14, 15, 18, 24
 aftermath of the battle 87, **88**
 at Bouvines 35, 53, 62–64, 66, 73, 78–79, 81, 86
 northern campaign 50–52
 financing and organizing the armies 26–31
Flanders 6, 13–14, 17, 18
Flemings 30, 57, 67, 71, 89
foot soldiers 35, 36–37, 39
 at Bouvines 41, 73, **74–76**, 78–79, 81–85, 86
France, John 59–60
Friedrich II of Germany 12–13, 16, 87

Galon de Montigny 65, 73, **74–76**
Gautier de Châtillon, Count of Saint-Pol 21, 62–63, **65**, 65–66, 69, 72–73, 78–79, 88–89
Gautier des Ghistelle 66, 68, 69
Geoffroi, Count of Anjou 5, 16
Gérard la Truie 65, 80
Guérin, 'Brother' 10, 18–19, 31
 at Bouvines 55–56, 58–63, 65–67, 69, 85, 88
Guillaume de Barres 14, 65, 70, 80
Guillaume le Breton 18, 19, 22, 24, 25, 33–34, 37, 41
 aftermath of the battle 87, 88
 at Bouvines 52, 54–61, 64–69, 71–73, 77, 80–81, 84–86
Gesta Philippi Augusti 52, 58–59, 61, 65–69, 71–73, 77, 80–81, 85–87
 northern campaign 51–52
Philippide 24, 52, 60, 61, 67, 71, 77, 81
 southern campaign 44, 45–49

Heinrich VI, Emperor 12, 20
helmets 31–32
Hendrik, Duke of Limburg 15, 16, 66
Hendrik I, Duke of Brabant 14–16, 26, 52, **52**, 55, 66, 70, 81
Henri, Count of Bar 21, 33, 65
Henry II, King of England 5–6, 10, 16, 23, 28, 30, 36, 89
Henry III, King of England 58, 87, 92
heraldry 33, 39
horses 31, 33, 35, 68, 71, 76, 80, 85
Hugues, Bishop of Liège 15–16
Hugues de Boves 55, **73**, 81, 84

Innocent III, Pope 13, 91
Ireland 10–11, 12

Jeanne of Flanders 13
John, King of England 5–8, 10–12, 14, 17, 18, **29**, 49
 aftermath of the battle 87–88

 character and military background 10–12, 49
 consequences of Bouvines 89–92
 Magna Carta 90–92, **90–91**
 as paymaster 55
 plans and strategy 22–23
 southern campaign 42–49
 vassals 27, 28
jousting 34, **64**, 67, **67**, 68, 71

knights 30, 31–35, 40–41
Knights Hospitaller 18, 20

Liège 15
Lille 14, **54**, 54–55, 56
Louis, Count of Artois 18, 25, **25**, 44–45, 49, **49**, 87, 91–92
Louis VII, King of France 5, 17, 19
Louis VIII, King of France **19**, 87
Lusignan family 6, 44–45

Magna Carta 90–92, **90–91**
Mauvoisin, Pierre 65, 80
meeting engagement model of battle 59–60
Michel de Harmes 68, 69
Miervant castle 43, 44
militia 36, 64
Minstrel of Reims 57–58
Mortagne 52
mounted serjeants 35–36, 41, 55, 67–68, 69

Nantes 19, **44**, 45, 49
Normandy 5, 6, 10, 12, 14, 17, 18
northern campaign 23, 50–52, 53
Notre-Dame Cathedral **51**

orders of battle 39–41
organization and finance of armies 26–31
Otto IV, King of Germany and Emperor of Rome **12**, 12–16, 24, **61**
 aftermath of the battle 87
 at Bouvines 33, 54–55, 59–64, 67, **68**, 73, 77–81
 northern campaign 50–52, 53

Philip I of Flanders 13, 17
Philipp of Swabia 12–13
Philippe Augustus (King Philippe II of France) 5–8, 11–18, **57**, **64**, **66**, **73**, **89**
 at Bouvines, morning 54–58
 at Bouvines, afternoon deployment 58–66
 at Bouvines, afternoon battle 36, 67–81, 85–86
 aftermath of the battle 87–88, 89
 character and military background 16–18
 crusades 17, 18, 19, 20

northern campaign 50–52, 53
plans and strategy 25
saved from the foot soldiers 73, **74–76**
southern campaign 44–49
vassals 28, 57–58
Philippe de Dreux, Bishop of Beauvais 19–21, 61, **77**, 78–79, 80
pitched battles 23–24, 25, 34–35, 37, 49, 52, 55
plans and strategy 22–25, 88–89
Poitou 5, 6, 8, 22, 25, 41, 42–45, 49, 87

raids and counter-raids 24, **24**, 25, 34
Renaud de Dammartin, Count of Boulogne 14, **14**, 19, 24, 81
aftermath of the battle 87
at Bouvines 31, 55, 61–63, 71, 77–79, 82–86, 89
character of 14, 55
northern campaign 50–52, 53
Richard I, King of England (Richard the Lionheart) 5, 6, **6**, 10–12, 14, 16, 64
crusades 17, 19, 20
and Philippe Augustus 17–18, 19, 20
Robert I de Dreux 19, 21
Robert II de Dreux 19, 21, **21**
at Bouvines 61, 62–63, 77, 78–79
Robert III de Dreux 18, 19, 21, 45, 61, 87
Robert of Béthune 52
Roche-aux-Moines castle siege 45–49
Roger of Wendover 12, 33, 37, 44, 55, 68

Saint-Omer 13–14, 18
set piece model of battle 60, 88
shields 32–33, **39**, **46–48**, 49, 68, 70
siege warfare 16–17, 18, 24, 45–49
southern campaign 22–23, 42–49
St Peter's Church, Bouvines 56, **56**, 57, **66**
standards 61, 64, 65, 73, **74–76**
Staufen dynasty 12–13, 16
stipendiaries 29, 67
strategy 22–25, 88–89
supply lines 24, 25, 45

Thomas de Saint-Valéry 21, 78–79, 80, 86
Tournai 14, 36, 51, **51**, 53, 56, 57
tournaments 34, 65, 68, 71, **72**
training, military 34, 39
Tristan, Pierre 73, **74–76**
troops 31–38
crossbowmen 37, **46–48**, 57
foot soldiers 35, 36–37, 39, 73, **74–76**, 78–79, 81–85, 86
mounted serjeants 35–36, 41, 55, 67–68, 69
numbers 40–41
orders of battle 39–41
salaried soldiers 28–31, 36
vassals 26–28, 29, 38–39, 57–58
see also knights

Valenciennes 50, 51, **51**
Verbruggen, Jan F. 39–41, 60, 66

Vermandois 25, 44, 50
Vexin 17, 20, 36
Vouvant 43, 44, 45

waged soldiers 28–31, 36
Waleran, Count of Luxembourg 66, 81
warfare, medieval **24**, 88
ambushes 56–57, **56**
escalade **44**
meeting engagement model 59–60
motivation for 38–39
organization and finance of armies 26–31
pitched battles 23–24, 25, 34–35, 37, 49, 52, 55
raids and counter-raids 24, 24, 25, 34
set piece model of battle 60, 88
siege warfare 16–17, 18, 24, 45–49
weapons **37–38**, **70**, 71, **74–76**, 81
crossbows 37, **38**, 45, **46–48**, 49, 57
daggers 33–34, **34**, 70, **70**, 80, 85, 86
lances 33, 34, 36, **52**, 68, 71, 72, 73
spears 36, 37, **38**, 79, 81, 84
swords 33, **38**, **68**, **69**, 71, 72, 81, 85
William Longespée, Earl of Salisbury **15**, 16, 19, 24
at Bouvines 55, 61, 62–63, **77**, 78–79, 86
aftermath of the battle 87